THE AVENGERS

THE ULTIMATE GUIDE TO EARTH'S MIGHTIEST HEROES!

LONDON, NEW YORK, MELBOURNE,
MUNICH AND DELHI

Project Editor Victoria Taylor
Editor Shari Last
Designer Nick Avery
Senior Art Editor Guy Harvey
Brand Manager Robert Perry
Design Manager Ron Stobbart
Publishing Manager Catherine Saunders
Art Director Lisa Lanzarini
Publisher Simon Beecroft
Publishing Director Alex Allan
Senior Production Editor Jennifer Murray
Production Controllers Man Fai Lau and Shabana Shakir

This edition published in 2014
First published in Great Britain in 2012 by
Dorling Kindersley Limited
80 Strand, London WC2R 0RL

013-181683-Apr/2012

A CIP catalogue record for this book
is available from the British Library.

ISBN: 978-0-2411-8656-5

Colour reproduction by Altaimage
Printed and bound in China by Hung Hing

The publisher would like to thank Alan Cowsill, Alastair Dougall
and Julia March for their editorial assistance; Chelsea Alon, Rich
Thomas, Scott Piehl and Lauren Kressel from Disney Publishing;
Ruwan Jayatilleke and Kelly Lamy from Marvel.

marvel.com
© 2014 MARVEL

THE AVENGERS
THE ULTIMATE GUIDE TO EARTH'S MIGHTIEST HEROES!

Written by Scott Beatty, Alan Cowsill, & Alastair Dougall

contents

The original art from page 19 of
The Avengers #58 (November 1968)
by John Buscema and George Klein.

As it appeared on the final printed page.

FOREWORD

"And there came a day... when Earth's Mightiest Heroes found themselves united against a common threat. On that day, the Avengers were born—to fight the foes no single Super Hero could withstand!"

It's all there in the top copy—that brief legend, composed in the 1970s, that ran at the start of every issue, briefly summing up the premise of the series for new readers who might have come to the comic book unaware.

That's the essence of most Super Hero team comics, but the Avengers embody that idea more strongly than anybody else. Not a family, not a persecuted minority, not grouped together by geography or gathered by the government, the Avengers are the Avengers because they want to be—because they need to be—in order to safeguard the world. They're the varsity, the biggest hitters, and the greatest players. A dynasty, one that every Super Hero secretly yearns to become a part of.

From a publishing perspective, it's also a very simple formula: all of the most popular characters together in a single magazine. Irresistible to any buyer who likes as few as two of them. And what reader doesn't fantasize about his favorite heroes meeting one another? Would they get along? Would they fight? What would happen? That's the key to the appeal of the idea. That and the notion of getting more heroes for your money, and typically in bigger, more epic adventures than are required of a single costumed do-gooder.

With a major motion picture on the horizon, the first film of its kind to combine the stars and casts of several other successful Super Hero movies in one picture, the concept of the Avengers is about to be transplanted to another medium, where millions of viewers will doubtless fall victim to its spell. And why not? It promises to be the biggest and most spectacular Super Hero adventure ever filmed!

I've edited *Avengers* for longer than any other person, a tenure that's fourteen years long at the time of this writing. So I feel a very personal connection to the series. If this is your first encounter with the Avengers, welcome—everything you need to know is on the pages that follow. And if you're someone who's already encountered the team, whether in comics or elsewhere:

"Heed the call—for now, the Avengers Assemble!"

Tom Brevoort
Editor, *The Avengers*

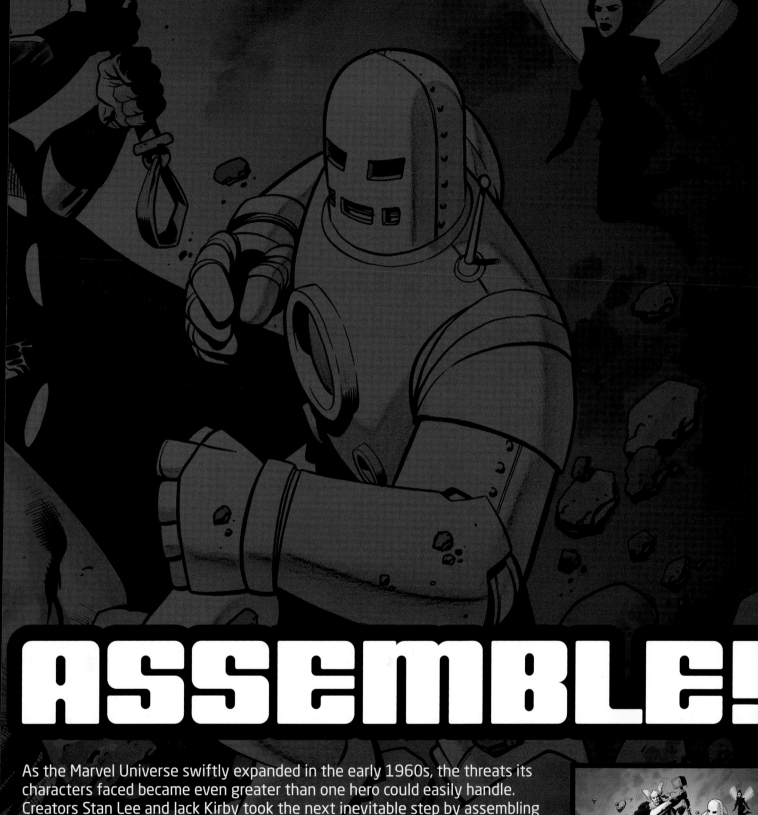

ASSEMBLE!

As the Marvel Universe swiftly expanded in the early 1960s, the threats its characters faced became even greater than one hero could easily handle. Creators Stan Lee and Jack Kirby took the next inevitable step by assembling a team of characters hailed in cover copy as "Earth's Mightiest Heroes!" *The Avengers* gathered Marvel's heaviest hitters under a single banner, soon to become the company's flagship title for decades to follow!

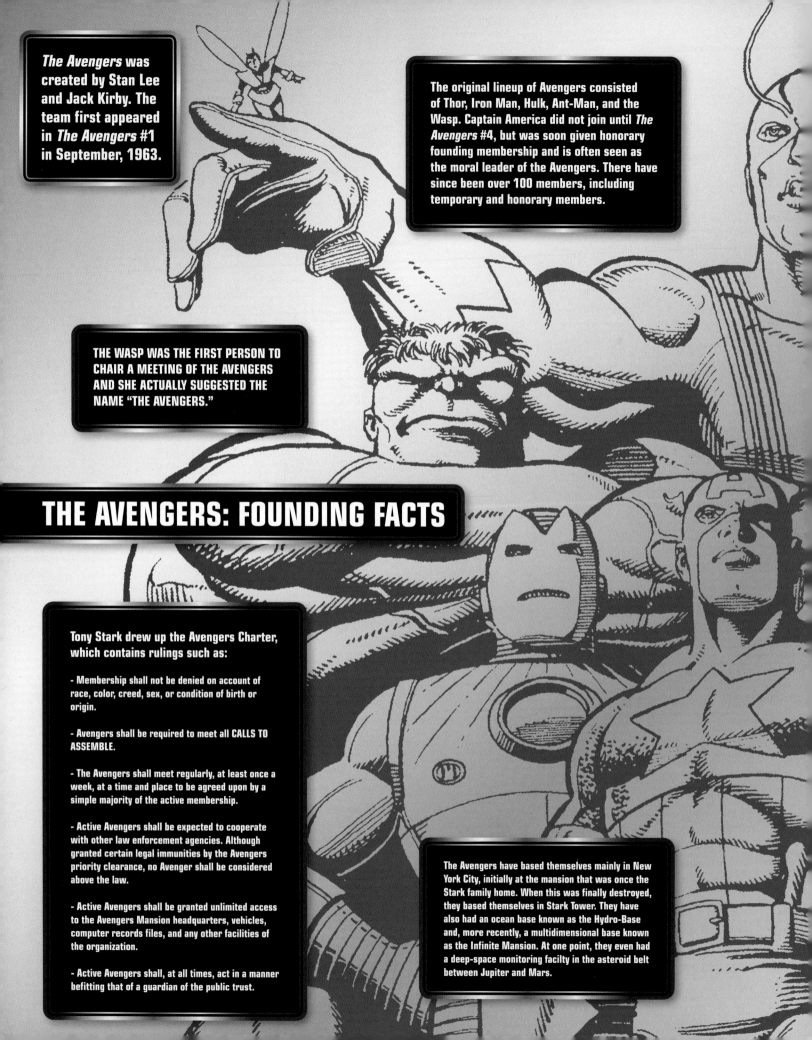

The Avengers was created by Stan Lee and Jack Kirby. The team first appeared in *The Avengers* #1 in September, 1963.

The original lineup of Avengers consisted of Thor, Iron Man, Hulk, Ant-Man, and the Wasp. Captain America did not join until *The Avengers* #4, but was soon given honorary founding membership and is often seen as the moral leader of the Avengers. There have since been over 100 members, including temporary and honorary members.

THE WASP WAS THE FIRST PERSON TO CHAIR A MEETING OF THE AVENGERS AND SHE ACTUALLY SUGGESTED THE NAME "THE AVENGERS."

THE AVENGERS: FOUNDING FACTS

Tony Stark drew up the Avengers Charter, which contains rulings such as:

- Membership shall not be denied on account of race, color, creed, sex, or condition of birth or origin.

- Avengers shall be required to meet all CALLS TO ASSEMBLE.

- The Avengers shall meet regularly, at least once a week, at a time and place to be agreed upon by a simple majority of the active membership.

- Active Avengers shall be expected to cooperate with other law enforcement agencies. Although granted certain legal immunities by the Avengers priority clearance, no Avenger shall be considered above the law.

- Active Avengers shall be granted unlimited access to the Avengers Mansion headquarters, vehicles, computer records files, and any other facilities of the organization.

- Active Avengers shall, at all times, act in a manner befitting that of a guardian of the public trust.

The Avengers have based themselves mainly in New York City, initially at the mansion that was once the Stark family home. When this was finally destroyed, they based themselves in Stark Tower. They have also had an ocean base known as the Hydro-Base and, more recently, a multidimensional base known as the Infinite Mansion. At one point, they even had a deep-space monitoring facilty in the asteroid belt between Jupiter and Mars.

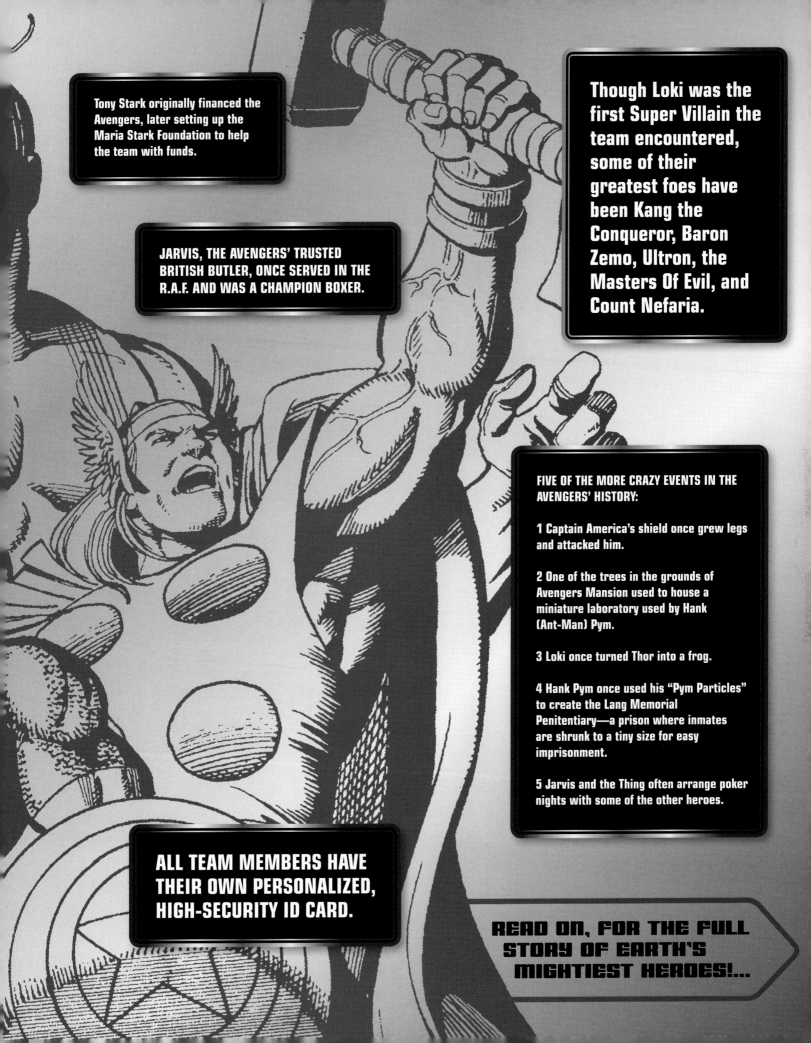

Tony Stark originally financed the Avengers, later setting up the Maria Stark Foundation to help the team with funds.

Though Loki was the first Super Villain the team encountered, some of their greatest foes have been Kang the Conqueror, Baron Zemo, Ultron, the Masters Of Evil, and Count Nefaria.

JARVIS, THE AVENGERS' TRUSTED BRITISH BUTLER, ONCE SERVED IN THE R.A.F. AND WAS A CHAMPION BOXER.

FIVE OF THE MORE CRAZY EVENTS IN THE AVENGERS' HISTORY:

1 Captain America's shield once grew legs and attacked him.

2 One of the trees in the grounds of Avengers Mansion used to house a miniature laboratory used by Hank (Ant-Man) Pym.

3 Loki once turned Thor into a frog.

4 Hank Pym once used his "Pym Particles" to create the Lang Memorial Penitentiary—a prison where inmates are shrunk to a tiny size for easy imprisonment.

5 Jarvis and the Thing often arrange poker nights with some of the other heroes.

ALL TEAM MEMBERS HAVE THEIR OWN PERSONALIZED, HIGH-SECURITY ID CARD.

READ ON, FOR THE FULL STORY OF EARTH'S MIGHTIEST HEROES!...

THE AVENGERS
Vol.1 #1

> "BAH! This complicates things for me! I only want to find a way to lure Thor up here! I'm not interested in those others!"
> **Loki**

Main Characters: Thor; Iron Man; Hulk; Ant-Man; the Wasp

Main Supporting Characters: Rick Jones and the Teen Brigade; Jane Foster

Main Locations: New York City; the Isle of Silence (Asgard); the American Southwest

Publication Date
September 1963

Editor-in-chief
Stan Lee

Cover artists
Jack Kirby, Dick Ayers

Writer
Stan Lee

Penciler
Jack Kirby

Inker
Dick Ayers

Colorist
Uncredited

BACKGROUND

In the "real world," the formation of the Avengers was a no-brainer. Since the solo Super Hero books were enjoying great sales success, Marvel Comics increased its line of monthly titles to match growing demand. One of the first new releases was an answer to many fans' requests to see their favorite characters join forces! So why not assemble a comic book with Earth's Mightiest Heroes under a single banner? Writer Stan Lee and artist Jack Kirby re-teamed on *The Avengers*, a title that brought together their fastest rising stars, starting with Thor, Ant-Man (and the Wasp), Hulk, and Iron Man, and would soon include nearly the entire rapidly-expanding Marvel Universe!

The Story

Exiled to Asgard's barren Isle of Silence, trickster Loki was imprisoned in body, but his malicious mind was free to engineer a disaster to draw his hated brother Thor back to Asgard and plan the Thunder God's DOOM!

1

2

3

4

5

6 **7**

Loki's great jealousy of Thor fueled his unceasing desire for revenge **(1)**. Loki knew that Thor was favored by their father Odin, King of the Norse Gods, and wanted to lure Thor back to Asgard where he might defeat him for all to see. Projecting his thoughts to Earth, Loki briefly pondered attacking Dr. Don Blake, Thor's human alter-ego, a physician who walked with a limp. But even cowardly Loki knew that humbling the stalwart God of Thunder himself was sweeter revenge than bullying a disabled doctor **(2)**. Casting his mind further, Loki searched for a menace formidable enough to force Blake to transform into Thor **(3)**. And he didn't need to look far.

Spying the Incredible Hulk, Loki cast an illusion upon a train trestle as the Green Goliath leaped past **(4)**. Hulk thought he saw a bundle of dynamite primed to explode and launched himself at the rails! Unfortunately, Hulk's nigh-invulnerable body smashed the tracks as a speeding locomotive loomed! Hulk used his own body to prop up the shattered rails and save the train, but the damage was done. Hulk was wrongly accused of causing the near-catastrophe.

Rick Jones knew Hulk wouldn't have intentionally destroyed the railroad so he and the Teen Brigade sent out a radio message in an attempt to obtain the Fantastic Four's help in clearing Hulk of wrongdoing. True to form, Loki intercepted the radio waves and diverted the broadcast, inadvertently splitting the message and transmitting it to Ant-Man, the Wasp, and the invincible Iron Man as well as Thor (his intended target) **(5)**! Reed Richards, the Fantastic Four's Mr. Fantastic, responded to the Teen Brigade, assuring the well-meaning youths that other heroes would help while the FF wrapped up another case **(6)**. Loki succeeded in tricking Thor into returning to Asgard after the Thunder God battled an illusory Hulk.

Elsewhere, the hounded Green Goliath hid in a traveling circus, disguising himself as Mechano, the most powerful life-like robot on Earth **(7)**! As Ant-Man, the Wasp, and Iron Man tried to help and subdue a defensive Hulk on Earth, Thor battled Loki on Asgard, grappling with a gaggle of giant trolls under Loki's thrall **(8)**! Ultimately besting Thor brought Loki to Earth and forced him to reveal his manipulations to the other heroes, who realized then that Hulk was blameless in the railroad mishap. Loki, however, would not accept defeat **(9)**. Turning his body lethally radioactive to frighten away the mortal heroes, Loki hoped to continue his battle with Thor uninterrupted. But the heroes, united in their determination to defeat the God of Deceit, pooled their powers to lure Loki into a lead-lined storage tank **(10)**! With Loki thus trapped, Earth's Mightiest Heroes realized the profound strength in their teaming and elected to continue as a united force for good. Thus, the Avengers came to be **(11)**!

> "I'm sick of bein' hunted and hounded. I'd rather be with you than against you! So whether you like it or not, I'm joinin' the... the... HEY! What are you callin' yourselves?"
>
> Hulk

9

8

10

11

THOR

CHARACTER

An Asgardian god cast down to Midgard in order to learn a lesson in humility, Thor more than made up for his hubris by becoming a hero to Earth and a founder member of the Avengers!

Monsters and mortals, be warned! The Odinson would have words with you!

Prince of Asgard

For Thor, pride came before a fall from grace and earned him temporary banishment from Asgard, home to the Norse Gods. Stripped of his godhood and made to walk among mankind not only as a human but as a disabled one—Dr. Donald Blake—the God of Thunder learned his lesson. He grew to love and respect the mortals who had once worshipped his kind. During his time in Blake's guise, Thor at first had no memory of his own thunderous power.

A subconscious urging from his father Odin, king of the Norse Gods, eventually led Blake to Norway, where he struck his walking stick against a boulder and transformed back into his godly form in time to thwart alien Kronan invaders. Thereafter, Thor used his restored powers wisely, eventually taking his place as one of Earth's Mightiest Heroes. He won back the respect of his father and was permitted to return to his rightful place among the Asgardian immortals. But ever after, Thor has found himself drawn to Earth and the protection of its many peoples who have come to regard him as one of the planet's most trusted guardians. This Prince of Asgard was one of the first Avengers and remains a loyal member even when called away to conflicts in other realms. Thor's indefatigable strength and warrior's spirit are much admired by his teammates, who know that the sound of thunder is nothing less than the hammer strike of one of the Avengers' most powerful members!

Asgard, the otherdimensional home of the Norse Gods, was connected to Earth (Midgard) by a rainbow bridge. It was destroyed during the apocalyptic event known as Ragnarok. A new earthbound Asgard has now been built.

For Thor's adopted brother Loki, sibling rivalry soon turned to brotherly hate that spilled beyond Asgard and threatened Earth itself!

As Dr. Donald Blake, Thor fell in love with nurse Jane Foster. Jane briefly became an Asgardian, but could not cope with her powers and was sent back to Earth minus her memories of Thor.

Immensely strong, Thor is one of the few beings capable of lifting the enchanted hammer Mjolnir. He wields it in battle against a host of adversaries, including the Frost Giants of Jotunheim, sworn enemies of Asgard and its gods.

Donald Blake transformed from man to god by striking his stick upon the ground, thus summoning the hammer Mjolnir and the powers of Thor.

14

Thor wears traditional viking armor.

Iron gauntlets protect Thor from the elemental forces unleashed by Mjolnir.

Mjolnir's inscription reads: "Whosoever holds this hammer, if he be worthy, shall possess the power of... THOR."

Thor's Belt of Strength doubles his brawn.

"THE OTHER AVENGERS ARE MORTAL AS THOU SAYEST— BUT I AM FAR MORE!"

KEY DATA

REAL NAME Thor Odinson

OCCUPATION Prince of Asgard, God of Thunder

AFFILIATIONS Norse Gods of Asgard, the Avengers

POWERS/WEAPONS Thor possesses the strength and endurance of a god, and has a greatly extended life span. He is immortal as long as he eats a Golden Apple of Iduun from time to time. His body is many times denser than that of a human—he is highly resistant to injury and immune to most diseases. Thor can fly at supersonic speeds within Earth's atmosphere and faster than the speed of light when in space. His beserker rages increase his strength as he gets more and more angry.

MJOLNIR
Forged from nigh-unbreakable uru metal, the enchanted hammer Mjolnir allows its wielder to call down wind, rain, thunder, and lightning. Thor can summon Mjolnir mentally and channel his powers through it to strike devastating blows or blasts of energy. By spinning Mjolnir at incredible speeds, he can also open portals to other dimensions.

Would the Avengers exist without Thor? If not for his stepbrother Loki's machinations against him, the team might never have assembled at all.

15

HULK

CHARACTER

Bruce Banner's angry alter-ego, the Incredible Hulk, was the Avengers' first quarry. The team's raison d'etre after Loki set several heroes on a collision course with Hulk, he is now one of their major foes.

Inexhaustible and nearly invulnerable, Hulk is also virtually unstoppable. The madder he gets, the more powerful he becomes, even increasing in mass and size like a jade juggernaut!

Green with Anger

Physicist Dr. Robert Bruce Banner was developing an experimental Gamma Bomb at a top-secret government research facility when teenager Rick Jones wandered onto the test site minutes before the Gamma Bomb's detonation. Banner rushed to save him by pushing Jones into a shelter, but was himself bombarded by the full measure of gamma radiation. The even-tempered physicist's body was changed at the cellular level, imbued with gamma-irradiated power unleashed in moments of stress or anger. During those times, Banner mutated into a Green Goliath dubbed "the Incredible Hulk." Though initially at odds with the heroes who would soon form the Avengers, Hulk joined the team rather than fight them. His membership was short-lived, but the issue of his alter-ego continued as Banner struggled for years to cure or control the Hulk within. At best, Hulk has been a hero, defending Earth from countless threats. At worst, the Green Goliath has been a menace to society. He launched a "World War Hulk" against the heroes he blamed for his woes, including his former Avengers teammates.

Hulk was gray in his debut due to a print error.

The love of Banner's life is Betty Ross. They married, but she was later poisoned by the Abomination. Her father, Thunderbolt, put Betty in cryonic suspension until the Leader and MODOK turned her into Red She-Hulk.

Bruce Banner saved Rick Jones from certain annihilation, a debt that Jones has struggled to repay ever since.

After Hulk first left the Avengers, he allied himself with Namor the Sub-Mariner to attack the team. Since then, Hulk's ties to the team have been tenuous at best. When Banner controls his raging Id, Hulk has been a powerful ally. When Hulk is fully in control, all bets are off!

Don't make him mad! At first, Banner transformed into the Incredible Hulk only at night. Soon, any form of stress would release the Green Goliath!

Hulk nearly conquered Earth after defeating the Avengers and routing the U.S. Army. He even forced the Illuminati to battle each other in a gladiatorial arena.

Hulk's aging is slowed, or may have ceased altogether, due to the regenerative properties of his gamma ray irradiated cells.

Hulk can leap many miles in a single bound.

Hulk has an innate ability to home in on the site of his original exposure to the explosive energies of the Gamma Bomb.

Able to adapt to virtually any environment, Hulk can survive underwater or in airless space indefinitely!

KEY DATA

REAL NAME Robert Bruce Banner

OCCUPATION Scientist

AFFILIATIONS Avengers, Defenders, Fantastic Four, Pantheon, Horsemen of the Apocalypse, Warbound.

POWERS/WEAPONS Possesses limitless strength and endurance. Hulk's transformed body can quickly regenerate from any injury.

ANGER MANAGEMENT
Bruce Banner has tried every conceivable method, including meditation and psychiatry, to control the Hulk. However, multiple personalities springing forth from childhood trauma and abuse may have given rise to the Green Goliath in the first place.

"YES, HULK WAS AVENGER ONCE... DIDN'T LIKE IT!"

Banner's transformations into Hulk have resulted in several personalities, including the gray-skinned Joe Fixit and the brilliant Maestro with darker green skin and the distinction of having made himself master of the world.

17

IRON MAN

CHARACTER

Tony Stark once built tools of war. And what is Iron Man's armor if not a weapon of mass destruction? For Tony Stark, the armor was first the means to save his life. Soon it would save his soul—and the world.

Tony once needed the armor to stay alive, but that errant piece of shrapnel is now long gone. The most recent "Extremis" Iron Man armor is mentally controlled, composed of liquid metal stored in his hollowed out bones!

The Man in the Iron Mask

Genius Tony Stark inherited a controlling interest in Stark Industries when his parents, Howard and Maria Stark, died in a car crash. While consulting with the U.S. military in Afghanistan, he was injured when his convoy struck a Stark Industries landmine. With shrapnel lodged dangerously near his heart, Tony was living on borrowed time. Taken prisoner by Afghan insurgents, he worked with fellow prisoner and inventor Ho Yinsen to build a primitive Iron Man armor with an electromagnetic chestplate to keep the shrapnel from destroying his heart. Following his escape and return to the U.S., Tony refined his life-saving armor and decided that Stark Industries would no longer make weapons of war. Iron Man was going to do everything in his power to make the world a better place. Iron Man soon became one of the four founding members of the Avengers, which Tony funded through the Maria Stark Foundation. The team based themselves in Stark Mansion, renamed Avengers Mansion. Iron Man would be the Avengers' heart and soul in the years to come, even when Tony himself battled personal demons, including alcoholism and the hostile takeover of his company. Tony has often been the Avenger to reunite the team in times of dissolution and despair. While his teammates have not always approved of his politics regarding the role of Super Heroes in the world, all would agree that beneath Iron Man's unyielding armor beats a heart of gold.

To prevent the shrapnel from moving and further damaging his heart, Tony and Ho Yinsen devised a magnetic field generator inside an armor chestplate.

Iron Man's first appearance saw him battle the Viet-Cong during the Vietnam War!

A notorious ladies' man, Tony Stark remains a bachelor to this day.

Upgrade or die. That's the maxim of any forward-thinking engineer. And Tony Stark is no different, employing a whole arsenal of Iron Man armors for different missions.

There is a global arms race for high-tech armor. Iron Man has faced a host of foes like Whiplash, Titanium Man, and Crimson Dynamo who have reverse-engineered Iron Man technology to build their own armored bodysuits.

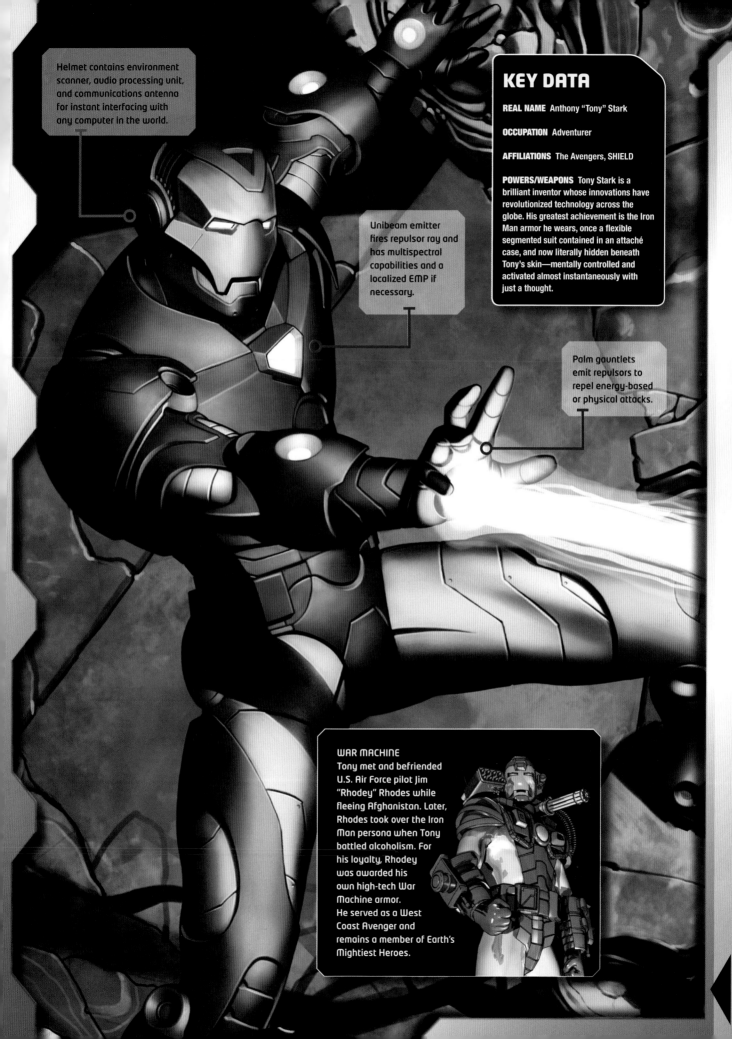

Helmet contains environment scanner, audio processing unit, and communications antenna for instant interfacing with any computer in the world.

Unibeam emitter fires repulsor ray and has multispectral capabilities and a localized EMP if necessary.

Palm gauntlets emit repulsors to repel energy-based or physical attacks.

KEY DATA

REAL NAME Anthony "Tony" Stark

OCCUPATION Adventurer

AFFILIATIONS The Avengers, SHIELD

POWERS/WEAPONS Tony Stark is a brilliant inventor whose innovations have revolutionized technology across the globe. His greatest achievement is the Iron Man armor he wears, once a flexible segmented suit contained in an attaché case, and now literally hidden beneath Tony's skin—mentally controlled and activated almost instantaneously with just a thought.

WAR MACHINE
Tony met and befriended U.S. Air Force pilot Jim "Rhodey" Rhodes while fleeing Afghanistan. Later, Rhodes took over the Iron Man persona when Tony battled alcoholism. For his loyalty, Rhodey was awarded his own high-tech War Machine armor. He served as a West Coast Avenger and remains a member of Earth's Mightiest Heroes.

"I WENT FROM BEING A MAN TRAPPED IN AN IRON SUIT TO BEING A MAN FREED BY IT."

Since first donning the Iron Man armor, Tony Stark depended on the power of technology to keep him alive. Now that Iron Man is quite literally part of him, the armor as much within him as without, one might wonder if Tony has also surrendered a portion of his humanity to bond more fully with Iron Man.

19

HANK PYM

CHARACTER

Henry "Hank" Pym discovered Pym Particles, enabling him to shrink to insect size or become a towering giant. He first became the hero Ant-Man, but the gaudy suits Hank wore as his many aliases hid a troubled soul.

Hank briefly retired from the heroic life before re-emerging as Goliath. As Goliath, he could grow to 25 feet, but only maintain this height for 15 minutes—a problem during longer bouts of fighting for the Avengers.

A lab accident brought about a personality change and, as Yellowjacket (left), Hank married Janet. He fought crime in this guise until insecurities blighted his marriage and Avengers career.

Better suited to research than to crime-fighting, Hank found a fulfilling role as the West Coast Avengers' scientific advisor and HQ manager.

The Life of Pym

Henry Pym started out as the Man in the Ant Hill being chased by bees and ants.

Biochemist Henry "Hank" Pym swore to battle injustice following the death of his wife, Maria. He then invented Pym Particles and became Ant-Man. A founder member of the Avengers, Hank fought Super Villains alongside his new partner, Janet Van Dyne, a scientist's daughter who bore a strong resemblance to his first wife. Janet used Pym Particles to become the Wasp. The wealthy, fun-loving, affectionate Janet and the repressed, workaholic scientist were an unusual partnership, but all went well for a while. Frustrated at being a tiny Super Hero, Hank adapted his formula to become Giant-Man, then Goliath, Yellowjacket and, briefly, the Wasp. Never at ease as a hero, Hank dabbled disastrously with robotics, accidentally creating the murderous robot Ultron, then cracked up and left Janet and the Avengers. Framed by the villain Egghead, he landed in jail.

Although rehabilitated, Hank has proved almost as unstable as his particles, his life complicated by his continuing feelings for his ex-wife Janet and guilt over his creation of the endlessly upgrading, genocidal Ultron, who has proved one of the Avengers—and humanity's—worst and most persistent foes. He is now running a school for young, would-be heroes, Avengers Academy.

Hank again took up the mantle of Giant-Man when he opened Avengers Academy, teaching superpowered delinquents how to control their powers and become heroes. His troubled past helped Hank empathize with the kids.

At first, Hank was unable to control his Pym Particle potion (top), but he soon showed those ants who was boss (above)!

Hank developed particles that enabled him to grow up to 100 feet tall. Becoming Giant-Man was good for crime-fighting, but a strain on Hank's health.

20

COSTUMED TRIBUTE
During the Skrulls' Secret Invasion of Earth, Hank was replaced by a Skrull. After the Skrulls' defeat, Hank returned to discover that his former wife Janet Van Dyne had been turned into a human bomb by his Skrull counterpart and had apparently been killed. Overcome with remorse, Pym paid tribute to her memory by adopting the Super Hero ID of the Wasp in the Mighty Avengers.

Ant-Man's helmet transmits psionic/electronic waves, enabling him to command colonies of ants to do his bidding.

"I REALIZED WHAT I BROUGHT TO THE TABLE. I, HENRY PYM WAS THE SMARTEST MAN IN THE ROOM..."

Although Hank Pym renounced his Ant-Man identity, the suit survived. Scott Lang donned it to save his daughter Cassie (now in the Young Avengers). With Pym's approval, Scott assisted the Fantastic Four and joined the Avengers. He was killed during the Scarlet Witch's attempt to disassemble the team. The Ant-Man suit was then adopted by disreputable ex-SHIELD agent Eric O'Grady, who joined the Secret Avengers.

KEY DATA

REAL NAME Henry "Hank" Pym

OCCUPATIONS Biochemist, adventurer, manager of Avengers Compound, director of Avengers Academy

AFFILIATIONS The Avengers, West Coast Avengers, Mighty Avengers

POWERS/WEAPONS As the Wasp: Superhuman strength; flight capability; can fire energy blasts from hands.
As Ant-Man/Yellowjacket: Uses Pym Particles to reduce to ant size, or to microscopic size, if neccessary; helmet allows communication with ants.
As Giant-Man/Goliath: Uses Pym Particles to grow in size from 10 to 100 feet.

As time passed, Pym ingested so many Pym Particles he could change size at will.

21

THE WASP

She was the lone lady Super Hero among a quintet of gods, monsters, and scientists. She has the distinction of having named Earth's Mightiest Heroes and she often acted as the Avengers' morale booster.

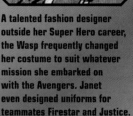

A talented fashion designer outside her Super Hero career, the Wasp frequently changed her costume to suit whatever mission she embarked on with the Avengers. Janet even designed uniforms for teammates Firestar and Justice.

The Wasp's first mision was to defeat the alien Pilai alongside Ant-Man.

Where Is Thy Sting?

Janet van Dyne never intended to become a Super Hero. But, then again, she never thought an alien Kosmosian would murder her father. Renowned scientist Vernon van Dyne used a gamma radiation beam to try and contact extraterrestrial life, bringing him into contact with Dr. Hank Pym, a handsome and brilliant young inventor. The beam came back with alien criminal Pilai in tow. Pilai had used the beam to escape his homeland and teleport to Earth whereupon he killed Janet's father. Janet told Hank Pym, who used his abilities as Ant-Man to help her stop Pilai from wreaking further harm. Pym shared his size-altering Pym Particles with Janet, gaining a crime-fighting partner when she shrinks to became the Wasp. Janet and Hank fell in love during their subsequent solo exploits, soon joining Thor, Iron Man, and Hulk to form the Avengers. Later, Hank and Janet were married, their nuptials witnessed by their Avengers teammates. The strains of a Super Hero marriage eventually proved too great for Janet and Hank, exacerbated by Hank's several mental breakdowns. Through it all, the Wasp found a home with the Avengers, her family in a life abuzz with adventure. The Wasp led the team through some of its most turbulent times, proving herself to both friend and foe. The tiniest Avenger perhaps believed in Earth's Mightiest Heroes more than any other.

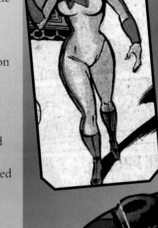

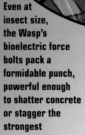
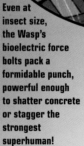

Hank Pym performed cellular surgery on Janet, giving her implants that led her to grow insectoid wings and antennae when she reduced in size.

Even at insect size, the Wasp's bioelectric force bolts pack a formidable punch, powerful enough to shatter concrete or stagger the strongest superhuman!

Pym Particles allow the Wasp to grow to gargantuan size as well as shrink to miniscule proportions. Janet has towered over her fellow Avengers as Giant-Girl!

During their stints as Avengers, Hank convinced his paramour Janet to hang up their costumes on several occasions, retiring to focus on Hank's research.

The Wasp's wings grow from her cellular implants when she reduces in size and are reabsorbed when she returns to normal.

Though rarely used, Janet possesses cellular implanted antennae that emerge when she shrinks, allowing her to control some hive-minded insects.

The Wasp trained in a variety of combat methods and martial arts with Captain America as her teacher.

DEATH OF THE WASP
During the Skrull's Secret Invasion of Earth, the Wasp ingested a growth serum spiked by Skrull Queen Veranke. To prevent Janet from becoming an unwitting explosive bioweapon, Thor used his hammer to repel her destructive energies back at her, saving many lives, but dooming the Wasp.

KEY DATA

REAL NAME Janet van Dyne

OCCUPATION Adventurer

AFFILIATIONS The Avengers

POWERS/WEAPONS The Wasp can fly at speeds of up to 40 mph. She can alter her size via Pym particles, shrinking to the size of an insect or growing into a giantess. The Wasp is able to emit bioelectric blasts capable of stunning most opponents into submission. The unique properties of Pym Particles also increase Janet's strength the smaller she becomes.

As the first female Avenger, the Wasp was often cast in the role of peacemaker between her male teammates, each jostling for primacy in the fledgling team. She served as the first female chairperson through two notable terms thanks to her long experience as one of Earth's Mightiest Heroes.

LOKI

"WHY DO PEOPLE ALWAYS ASSUME I'M LYING?"

Orphaned Frost Giant Loki was adopted by Odin, ruler of the Norse Gods. Jealousy of Odin's own son, Thor, created a monster out of immortal Loki. The "God of Mischief" was born—and, eventually, so were the Avengers.

Loki's hatred of Thor drives his every scheme. Loki covets the throne of Odin and has forged alliances with many of Asgard's enemies to increase his powers and further his plots.

According to prophecy, Loki is fated to initiate Ragnarok, the so-called "Twilight of the Gods" and ultimate destruction of Asgard, a future he eagerly anticipates. Loki has come to believe that Earth and its costumed heroes are key players in this final drama.

Trickster Myths

Loki would gladly destroy Earth, Asgard, and the whole of creation to humiliate Thor!

Loki's small size, though comparable to that of an Asgardian god, was an embarrassment to his father, the Frost Giant Laufey. For that reason, Loki was kept hidden in a fortress within Jotunheim, realm of the Frost Giants until Laufey was slain battling Odin and the gods of Asgard.

Though Loki was raised as Odin's son, Loki harbored deep resentment for his brother Thor, whom Odin favored. However, Odin was steadfast in his vow to never to show favoritism during the siblings' near-constant conflicts. Loki's envy manifested as mischief and trickery, which he focused upon Thor, or those Thor held dear. Loki caused the handle of Thor's hammer, Mjolnir, to be shortened during its creation from mystical uru metal by Odin himself. In one popular tale, Loki played a trick upon his half-brother by cutting the beautiful golden hair of the swordmaiden Sif, beloved of Thor.

Enraged, Thor demanded that Loki restore Sif's golden tresses. Loki compelled the dwarves Brokk and Eitri to spin new hair for Sif, but refused them payment for their services. Paid nothing, the dwarves responded in kind by creating Sif's new hair from nothing, forging black hair from the night itself. Thor's affections for Sif—now and forever raven-haired—remained ardent.

Eventually, in a plot to draw Thor into battle on Asgard, Loki inadvertently caused the Avengers' formation.

Odin once imprisoned Loki in an enchanted tree until someone shed a tear for him. Loki made a leaf fall in the eye of Heimdall, guardian of the rainbow bridge Bifrost. Heimdall's accidental tear allowed Loki to escape!

Loki has assumed the appearance of both friends and foes of Thor, including Lady Sif (above). After Loki was betrayed by ally Norman Osborn and killed by the Void, Thor resurrected him in the body of a child (right), probably to teach Loki a lesson, or to give him a chance to finally mature in both body and mind.

Loki's devious mind has crafted many complex stratagems in his attempts to thwart Earth's Mightiest Heroes and spark Ragnarok.

Styled to intimidate his opponents and stand above his fellow Asgardians, Loki's gilded horns reveal his great and unabashed vanity.

Though Loki's own energies are considerable, he has often sought other means of power—such as the fabled Norn Stones and Thor's hammer, Mjolnir—to augment his abilities.

Loki's resplendent robes reveal his position as a member of the ruling family of Asgard.

KEY DATA

REAL NAME Loki Laufeyson

OCCUPATION God of Mischief; God of Evil

AFFILIATIONS Norse Gods; the Cabal

POWERS/WEAPONS Asgard's most powerful sorcerer, Loki also possesses great strength and stamina like his fellow Norse gods, but usually avoids physical combat and relies instead on trickery and deception. He can fly, move between dimensional realms, and change his shape and appearance at will.

SINISTER SORCERER
Loki's magical manipulations also include astral projection, energy blasts, illusion casting, teleportation, shapeshifting, telepathy, and hypnosis.

"KNEEL, GOD OF THUNDER. KNEEL. KNEEL BEFORE YOUR CONQUEROR. KNEEL, AS IS YOUR DESERT AND DESTINY, BEFORE LOKI..."

While Loki has never been much of a "team player," he joined Norman Osborne's Cabal to further his own ends. In addition to Osborn and Loki, the Cabal included Namor, the Hood, the White Queen, and Dr. Doom, all of whom were convinced by the God of Evil to invade Asgard!

CAPTAIN AMERICA RETURNS!

In the closing days of World War II, Captain America was cast into freezing waters after thwarting a destructive Nazi rocket. The iconic hero was frozen in suspended animation until the Avengers found and revived him to join their heroic ranks!

CAPTAIN AMERICA

"I CAN'T SURRENDER. I DON'T KNOW HOW!"

The super soldier who rallied the Allies during World War II possessed qualities that transcended his time. Since joining the Avengers, Cap has inspired the team in all of its incarnations.

During the war, Captain America's campaign against tyranny was aided by sidekick Bucky Barnes. Cap and Bucky were members of the wartime Invaders.

Cap's combat skills include proficiency in boxing, judo, and various other martial arts, all enhanced by the Super Soldier Serum.

Super Soldier

Steve Rogers was the original 98-pound weakling. When the Nazis stormed across Europe, he attempted to enlist in the U.S. military to help the war effort. But Rogers couldn't even pass the basic physical requirements. Undaunted, Rogers volunteered for a top-secret program designed to create the perfect fighting machine, which was dubbed "Project: Rebirth." Dosed with an untested Super Soldier Serum and bombarded with experimental "vita-rays," Rogers found his physique radically altered. That transformative shot in the arm remade Rogers from head to toe and raised him to the pinnacle of human physical perfection. Through advanced combat training, the newly dubbed Captain America hit the front lines and fought his way to victory. A Nazi spy killed the serum's inventor, leaving Rogers the sole super soldier. During World War II, Captain America inspired the heroes of his day to beat back the Nazis, earning him the enmity of such Nazi foes as the Red Skull and Baron Zemo. It was Zemo who did what no other villain could, apparently killing Cap near the close of the war when Cap sacrificed himself to stop an explosives-laden drone plane. The explosion hurled Cap into icy waters.

Cap's wartime exploits made other young people join the fight against the Axis!

Dr. Abraham Erskine's Super Soldier Serum increased Rogers' strength tenfold!

Cap belonged to a coalition of costumed adventurers known as the Invaders. The team included Cap, Bucky, Namor the Sub-Mariner, the Human Torch and Toro, the Whizzer, Miss America, Spitfire, and Union Jack.

Hitler originally gave Johan Shmidt a unique uniform with a hideous red skull mask. Later, after exposure to Dust of Death, Shmidt became a living Red Skull.

The Super Soldier Serum in his system saved Cap from a freezing death by putting his body in a state of suspended animation until the Avengers found him decades later.

THE SHIELD
Next to his own fighting-fit body, Captain America's most recognizable weapon is his red-white-and-blue shield. The shield is virtually indestructible. In a defensive posture it can deflect high-velocity projectiles. Hurled like an oversized discus, it smashes through anything it hits.

Cap's A-for-America cowl is Kevlar lined and bulletproof.

Cap's body armor is designed to be lightweight and permit maximum mobility.

Shield forged from a Vibranium composite alloy.

"I KNOW SO LITTLE ABOUT THIS NEW CROP OF COSTUMED FIGHTERS! MY BEST BET IS TO WATCH THEM IN ACTION —SEE HOW POWERFUL THEY REALLY ARE!"

KEY DATA

REAL NAME Steve Rogers

OCCUPATION Adventurer, SHIELD Operative, Avengers team leader

AFFILIATIONS The Avengers, the Invaders, All-Winners Squad, SHIELD

POWERS/WEAPONS Enhanced strength, speed, and endurance, as well as proficiency in many combat disciplines and martial skills. Cap's aim is unerring, whether with a weapon or his own invulnerable shield.

Though not a founding member of Earth's Mightiest Heroes, Captain America is thought of as "The First Avenger," since his much publicized (and propagandized) exploits during World War II. Cap's reputation served to inspire generations of costumed champions to come.

THE AVENGERS
Vol.1 #16

"Now you'll know what it means to challenge the mighty Avengers!"
Giant-Man

Main Characters: Iron Man; Giant-Man; the Wasp; Thor; Captain America

Main Supporting Characters: Namor the Sub-Mariner; Rick Jones; Edwin Jarvis; Happy Hogan

Main Locations: New York City; the Amazon jungle of South America; Switzerland

Publication Date
May 1965

Editor-in-Chief
Stan Lee

Cover Artists
Jack Kirby, Sol Brodsky

Writer
Stan Lee

Penciler
Jack Kirby

Inker
Dick Ayers

Colorist
Uncredited

BACKGROUND

Ironically, it wasn't Super Villains who forced the founding members out during the second publication year of *The Avengers*, but scrutinizing readers. Fans had begun to wonder how the heroes could be engaged in Avengers' business while simultaneously sorting through a multi-part epic in their own solo titles. Writer Stan Lee took these logistical conundrums seriously and his solution was to shake up the lineup of Earth's Mightiest Heroes, repopulating the book with characters not seen elsewhere in the Marvel Universe. Captain America replaced the old guard with new faces like Hawkeye, Quicksilver, and the Scarlet Witch, eliminating the need to explain how each teammate could be—in readers' minds—in two places at once!

The Story

Three new super-adventurers—including two formerly evil mutants and a one-time archer adversary—join an all-new lineup of Earth's Mightiest Heroes, led by Captain America!

1

2

3

4

5

6

7

8

9

10

11

Super Villain team Masters of Evil vowed to make mean streets out of midtown Manhattan, threatening to raze the city and injure countless civilians in their bid to take down the Avengers once and for all. Numbered among the Masters' members were the Black Knight, the Melter, and Asgardian adversaries, the Executioner and the Enchantress. The fetching Enchantress was the first of her insidious ilk to realize that the Masters of Evil might have the upper hand with Captain America missing in action from the Avengers while pursuing his arch-foe Baron Zemo in South America. Emboldened, the Masters struck!

The Melter turned his melting ray upon a nearby lamppost, reducing it to slag and promising to do the same to the remaining Avengers **(1)**.

To protect innocent lives and property from further collateral damage, Thor spun his hammer, Mjolnir, at unimaginable speeds creating a whirling vortex to trap the Black Knight and the Melter **(2)**. Little did the foes realize that the God of Thunder had opened a space warp to a bleak and unpopulated dimension **(3)**. Back in Manhattan, the Enchantress and the Executioner chose discretion over villainy, preferring not to face an angry mob of vengeful New Yorkers. The Avengers followed the remaining Masters to the other dimension and defeated them after the villains discovered that their abilities were subject to different natural laws and subsequently backfired on them **(4)**.

Meanwhile, deep in the Amazon jungle, Captain America gave Baron Zemo—killed in battle with Cap—a solemn funeral before beating back Zemo's remaining mercenary forces **(5)**. The attack destroyed Cap's jet and left the Avenger stranded in the jungle with his sidekick Rick Jones.

Later, at Avengers Mansion, the weary team were shocked to discover that their headquarters had been breached by the battling bowman known as Hawkeye **(6)**. The archer, once thought to be an adversary, captured butler Edwin Jarvis and beseeched the team to let him prove his worth for membership as one of Earth's Mightiest Heroes **(7)**. After allowing Hawkeye to join, the Avengers sought out even more new members to bolster their ranks. Namor the Sub-Mariner, still at odds with the surface world, declined the invitation to join **(8)**. But two former foes, Quicksilver and the Scarlet Witch—both previously belonging to Magneto's Brotherhood of Evil Mutants—answered the Avengers' call to heroism and were anxious to redeem themselves in the eyes of the world **(9)**. Of course, Captain America was stunned to find out that the team had gone through a radical restructuring in his absence **(10)**.

But in a hastily assembled press conference, Cap welcomed and introduced the newest Avengers to cheering onlookers **(11)**!

"It has to be this way! The ranks of the Avengers will always need replenishing! The old must give way to the new!"

Iron Man

HAWKEYE

"WHEN YOU TALK TO THE COPS ABOUT THIS, TELL 'EM HAWKEYE WAS THE GOOD GUY WILL YA? I DON'T NEED ANY MORE BAD PRESS."

Hawkeye may always shoot his arrows straight and true, but his costumed career began as a villain in a case of mistaken identity that would eventually steer him toward redemption with Earth's Mightiest Heroes.

When working for a fair, Clint watched Tony Stark become Iron Man and was inspired to become a Super Hero himself.

Straight Arrow

As a boy, orphan Clint Barton ran away to join a traveling carnival. The show's resident marksman, Trickshot, realized the boy's uncanny ability in archery while teaching him to wield a bow and arrow. Clint honed his archery skills until he was a master bowman. Inspired by the early exploits of Iron Man, Clint created a costume and trick arrows, becoming Hawkeye. While trying to thwart a robbery, the masked Hawkeye was mistaken for a burglar and fought the armored Avenger instead. On the run, Hawkeye fell under the influence of the then-rogue Black Widow, and committed crimes to impress her. Later, when the Avengers put out an open call for new members, Hawkeye broke into Avengers Mansion to prove his mettle to the team, hoping that Earth's Mightiest Heroes would believe that he had indeed reformed. Iron Man vouched for the ace archer, and he began a long and eventful career as an Avenger. Hawkeye gave up his bow and arrow a couple of times, briefly becoming Goliath, and later Ronin, before becoming Hawkeye again.

Despite breaking into Avengers Mansion, Hawkeye's sincerity impressed his old foe Iron Man.

As the founding Avengers departed on leaves-of-absence, Hawkeye was among a "Kooky Quartet" of new members.

Clint proved that he wasn't merely the world's greatest archer. As Hawkeye, he wielded a variety of weapons with the same expert grace as he wielded a bow and arrow.

Hawkeye was among the founding members of the Avengers West Coast team, which also included the Vision and Wonder Man.

Hawkeye perished defending the Earth from a Kree assault, but when the Scarlet Witch remade reality, Clint Barton was reborn. He took up the mantle of Ronin, becoming the leader of Earth's Mightiest Heroes.

Hawkeye frequently utilizes a Stark-built sky-cycle, which can travel at 380 mph. The aircraft can hover steadily even in strong winds, so Hawkeye's aim is true.

KEY DATA

REAL NAME Clinton "Clint" Barton

OCCUPATION Adventurer

AFFILIATIONS The Avengers, the Thunderbolts

POWERS/WEAPONS Hawkeye is one of the world's greatest archers, able to shoot a variety of trick arrows with unerring aim. He is also an expert martial artist and acrobat, skilled with bladed weapons, nunchakus, and other ninja paraphernalia.

Custom-made collapsible bows ideal for all of Hawkeye's arrows.

Perfectly balanced arrows made from a lightweight alloy.

Avengers communicator and touch-screen mini-computer.

HAWKEYE'S QUIVER
Hawkeye's most frequently employed trick arrows include the following specially designed heads: sonic, explosive-tip, smoke bomb, flare, acid, suction-tip, cable, bola, boomerang, net, putty, and cable—to name just a few.

"GO OUT, FIGHT HARD, SCREW UP. SAVE THE WORLD A FEW TIMES... JUST KEEP TAKING THE SHOTS, OKAY?"

Once an Avenger, ALWAYS an Avenger. Despite everything he's been through, Hawkeye was one of the trusted heroes handpicked by Steve Rogers to headline the new Avengers team based in Avengers Tower.

THE SCARLET WITCH

The Scarlet Witch is the daughter of the world's most evil mutant. She married an android and gave birth to twins that never really existed. Is it any wonder that this once trusted hero completely lost her mind?

Good Witch

The Scarlet Witch first appeared as a member of the Brotherhood of Evil Mutants.

Twin mutants Wanda and Pietro Maximoff were raised in Transia in Eastern Europe, hidden from their father, the master of magnetism, Magneto! Unfortunately, Magneto laid claim to his children as they approached adulthood, when Wanda's mutant hex powers made the superstitious Transians fear she was a witch. So Wanda called herself the Scarlet Witch when she and Pietro, the speedster Quicksilver, joined Magneto's Brotherhood of Evil Mutants to wage war on humanity. But Wanda and Pietro did not share Magneto's hatred for *homo sapiens* and soon fled the Brotherhood.

When the Avengers held a membership drive to replace its departing founding members, the Scarlet Witch and Quicksilver joined the team. Wanda remained a member for years, serving both the East and West Coast teams through good times and bad. However, as her hex abilities increased in power, Wanda's sanity diminished. She conjured imaginary children from her marriage with the Vision. Eventually, she lost both her faux offspring and her tentative hold on reality, whereupon the Scarlet Witch turned against her fellow Avengers, disassembling Earth's Mightiest Heroes with her chaos magicks and remaking the world into a reality where mutants rule over humans.

During her first adventure with the Avengers, Wanda helped the team defeat the Minotaur!

Transian villagers accused Wanda of being a witch and threatened to kill her and Pietro. Magneto saved them, but at first he hid the fact that he was their father.

Initially, Wanda's reality-altering hexes required line of sight with the object or person(s) she intended to affect, as well as focused concentration.

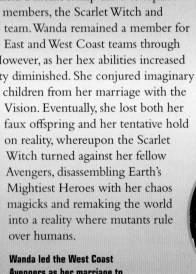

Wanda led the West Coast Avengers as her marriage to the Vision came to an end.

Wanda fell in love with her Avengers teammate the Vision. But when the synthezoid hero lost his ability to feel human emotions, their relationship faltered.

"LOOK AT US, DADDY! WE'RE FREAKS! MUTANTS! … YOU RUINED US! DADDY… NO MORE MUTANTS."

The Scarlet Witch's hexes create warps in probability, with devastating results.

The Scarlet Witch has normal strength for a woman of her height and build.

KEY DATA

REAL NAME Wanda Maximoff

OCCUPATION Adventurer

AFFILIATIONS The Avengers, the Brotherhood of Evil Mutants

POWERS/WEAPONS The Scarlet Witch's chaos magicks, her so-called "hexes," were once able to affect reality on a small scale, making random accidents happen at will in order to thwart opponents. As her mutant powers have grown through mystic study, she can—if properly motivated—affect reality on a grand scale, remaking the world around her into whatever she chooses.

Most recently, the Scarlet Witch resurfaced with amnesia in Latveria where she was engaged to Dr. Doom, who plotted to claim Wanda's chaos magick. But thanks to the X-Men and the Young Avengers, Doom failed on both counts.

35

QUICKSILVER

"HOW DO YOU CATCH THE WORLD'S FASTEST MAN?"

FAST & FURIOUS

Son of Magneto and twin brother of the Scarlet Witch, Pietro Django Maximoff first came to prominence as a maximum velocity member of his father's so-called Brotherhood of Evil Mutants. But Quicksilver, as hot-headed Pietro called himself, became disenchanted with Magneto's anti-human agenda and left the Brotherhood along with his twin sister. Determined to reform their ways, the siblings joined the Avengers during its first membership drive.

Pietro and Wanda Maximoff were born on Wundagore Mountain in the European country of Transia. Their mother gave birth to the mutants under the care of the High Evolutionary, who helped to hide them from evil Magneto by giving Pietro and Wanda to a Transian couple to be raised as their own.

Quite possibly the fastest mutant alive, Quicksilver can easily run rings around any opponent with his superspeed. He is able to generate cyclonic whirlwinds simply by running in circles.

TWIN POWERS

Pietro lost his superspeed on M-Day when twin Wanda depowered most of Earth's mutants. However, exposure to the Inhumans' Terrigen Mists restored Quicksilver's abilities. Despite the Scarlet Witch's repeated mental breakdowns, Pietro remains devoted to his sister and will always race to her defense. The twins' relationship with their father Magneto runs from hot to cold, depending on the mutant mastermind's manipulations of his estranged offspring.

"Hah, in his grief over his sister's plight, Pietro struck out at his old allies... And has forever alienated himself from the *homo sapiens*." Magneto

Quicksilver can beat a bolt of lightning conjured by Thor's enchanted hammer Mjolnir before it hits the ground. But his most unusual ability is limited time travel. Pietro can run fast enough to skip up to twelve days ahead in time. His top speed remains unclocked, and any adverse effects of the Terrigen Mists are yet to be revealed.

Cap's Kooky Quartet defeated Commissar, the gargantuan, superstrong dictator of Sin-Cong, an oppressive communist state. Its propagandist Commissar was revealed to be a robot, and the populace was freed from his iron grip!

When the Enchantress bewitched Power Man and used him to help discredit the Avengers, the team was branded a public menace and forced to disband! That is, until the Kooky Quartet tricked Power Man into revealing the Enchantress's deception. After Power Man was abandoned by his love, the smitten Super Villain surrendered—and then Cap quit!

KOOKY GANG

The founding Avengers sometimes needed a rest from superheroics and the demands of defending Earth from threats like the Masters of Evil. The solution was for the team to launch a membership drive and expand. Three former villains answered the call, each yearning to reform and prove their worthiness as Avengers. With Captain America leading, Hawkeye, Quicksilver, and the Scarlet Witch joined the team and the four became affectionately known as "Cap's Kooky Quartet." The Avengers' foes underestimated this untested lineup at their own peril. The "Kooky Quartet" soon proved that they were anything but kooky!

Captain America's leadership of the Kooky Quartet was frequently challenged by both Quicksilver and Hawkeye!

Kang launched a time-traveling attack on the Avengers, believing Cap's absence would let him defeat the vulnerable team. But when Cap rejoined his teammates in the far-flung future, Kang honored his word by ending the conflict (for now) and sending the Kooky Quartet back to their own era!

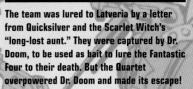

The team was lured to Latveria by a letter from Quicksilver and the Scarlet Witch's "long-lost aunt." They were captured by Dr. Doom, to be used as bait to lure the Fantastic Four to their death. But the Quartet overpowered Dr. Doom and made its escape!

Together with founding Avengers Hank Pym and the Wasp, the Kooky Quartet took on Prince Namor's aquatic adversary Attuma, who intended to inundate Earth with a flood-generating tidal-expander machine! Hawkeye used the team's Visi-Projector to locate his teammates and help them mop up Attuma and his Atlantean minions!

THE KOOKY QUARTET

"We'll live up to the proud tradition which [Iron Man], Thor, Giant-Man, and the Wasp have established! We'll never bring dishonor to our name!" **Captain America**

BARON ZEMO

"GUIDE MY HAND, FATHER—AS I AVENGE YOUR DEATH!"

One of the Avengers' most diabolical foes, Baron Zemo is the founder of the Super Villain team, Masters of Evil. Driven by a desire to destroy Captain America and the Avengers, Zemo will stop at nothing.

Helmut Zemo blames Cap for the death of his father and for his own horribly disfigured face.

Baron Zemo recruited the Black Knight, the Melter, and Radioactive-Man to form the first Masters of Evil.

History Repeats Itself

During World War II, Nazi scientist Heinrich Zemo threatened the Allies with his deadly weapons, including a "death ray" laser and "Adhesive X," an insoluble glue that could potentially stop advancing armies in their tracks. Ironically, Captain America showed Zemo just how sticky Adhesive X could be when he breached Zemo's secret lab and caused a vat of it to spill over the scientist, sticking his mask forever to his head. Zemo was finally killed during a confrontation with Captain America, only for his son—Helmut Zemo—to later assume the title of Baron Zemo. The new Zemo was also scarred by Cap and forced to wear his father's mask as he continued to seek revenge against the hero.

As Baron Zemo fired at Captain America, Cap threw his shield and shattered a vat of Adhesive X!

Baron Zemo used an experimental "Ionic Ray" to imbue Simon Williams with incredible strength.

The Avengers pursued the Baron when he kidnapped Rick Jones. A confrontation with Cap left Zemo buried beneath tons of rock!

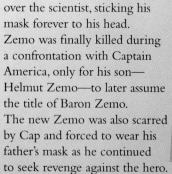

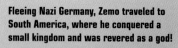

Fleeing Nazi Germany, Zemo traveled to South America, where he conquered a small kingdom and was revered as a god!

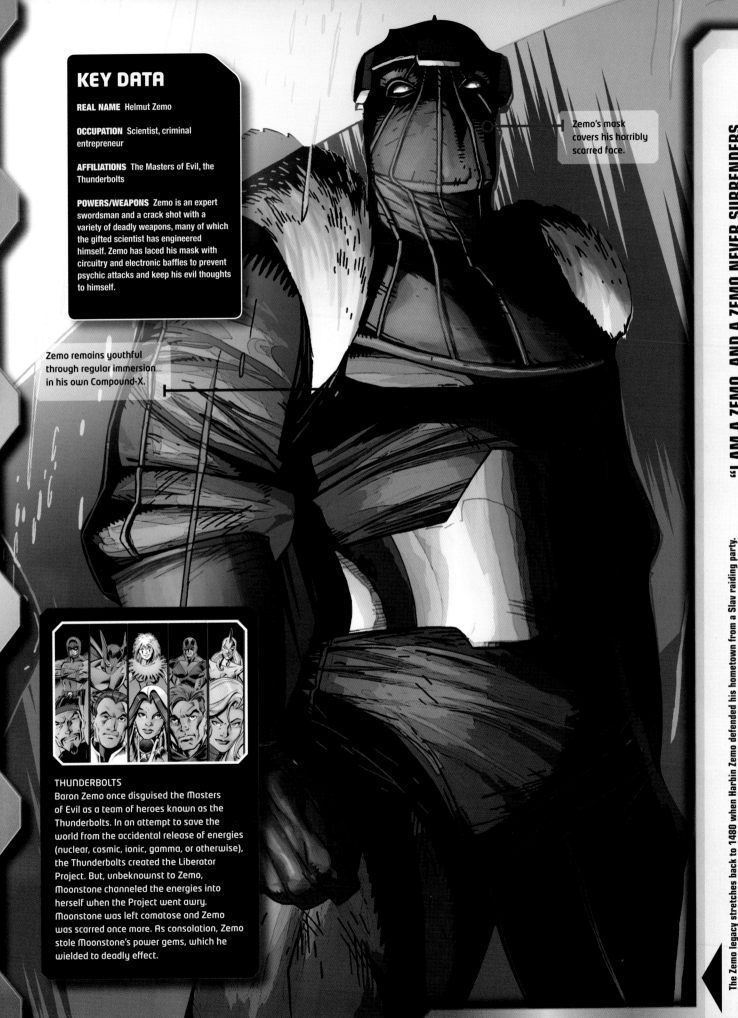

KEY DATA

REAL NAME Helmut Zemo

OCCUPATION Scientist, criminal entrepreneur

AFFILIATIONS The Masters of Evil, the Thunderbolts

POWERS/WEAPONS Zemo is an expert swordsman and a crack shot with a variety of deadly weapons, many of which the gifted scientist has engineered himself. Zemo has laced his mask with circuitry and electronic baffles to prevent psychic attacks and keep his evil thoughts to himself.

Zemo remains youthful through regular immersion in his own Compound-X.

Zemo's mask covers his horribly scarred face.

THUNDERBOLTS
Baron Zemo once disguised the Masters of Evil as a team of heroes known as the Thunderbolts. In an attempt to save the world from the accidental release of energies (nuclear, cosmic, ionic, gamma, or otherwise), the Thunderbolts created the Liberator Project. But, unbeknownst to Zemo, Moonstone channeled the energies into herself when the Project went awry. Moonstone was left comatose and Zemo was scarred once more. As consolation, Zemo stole Moonstone's power gems, which he wielded to deadly effect.

"I AM A ZEMO. AND A ZEMO NEVER SURRENDERS... IT IS MY DESTINY—MY BIRTHRIGHT—TO TRIUMPH."

The Zemo legacy stretches back to 1480 when Harbin Zemo defended his hometown from a Slav raiding party. Many of his descendants have desired power. Heinrich, despite his death, returned to face the Avengers as part of the Legion of the Unliving and his ghost once fought the Scarlet Witch. While his son at first followed in his father's footsteps, he later tried to use his power as a force for good and worked to redeem the Zemo name.

39

KANG

"TIME MEANS NOTHING TO KANG THE CONQUEROR!"

Kang is a time traveler from the distant future. Equipped with highly advanced technology, his obsession with the Avengers has given the team some of their strangest and deadliest adventures.

One verson of Kang disguised himself as Iron Man to kill the Avengers using a nuclear bomb. He succeeded but also destroyed the world.

King of Time

Kang first faced the Avengers as he sought to conquer the modern world.

Kang's real name is Nathaniel Richards and he is a distant descendent of Reed Richards' reality-traveling father. He was born on Earth-6311, a world where the Dark Ages never occurred and mankind had reached the moon by 900 CE. Born into an era of peace, Nathaniel studied the time-traveling records left by his namesake. He later found the original Nathaniel's citadel and his time machine, using the

Kang used his time machine to spend time in Ancient Egypt as Rama-Tut.

latter to adventure up and down the timestream. At one point Kang based himself in Ancient Egypt, where he took the name Rama-Tut and used his technology to become a god-like ruler. Kang had always been interested in Earth's Heroic Age, and became obsessed with the Avengers following defeat at their hands. His actions led to a multitude of Kangs spreading out across realities. The Prime Kang killed all his alternate versions until he alone remained.

Kang believed his futuristic weaponry would defeat the Avengers with ease.

The time traveler known as Immortus was a future version of Kang but the Time-Keepers split the two entities, making Kang's future his own.

Kang's wife Ravonna fell into a coma after being shot trying to save her husband.

Immortus and Kang fought each other across time, despite Immortus being a future incarnation of Kang.

A 16-year-old Kang traveled back in time and formed the Young Avengers as Iron Lad.

KEY DATA

REAL NAME Nathaniel Richards

OCCUPATION Conqueror, pharoah

AFFILIATIONS Former member of the Council of Kangs, the Cross-Time Kangs

POWERS/WEAPONS Kang ages at a slower rate than modern humans and his body is more resistant to radiation than people from earlier times. An expert strategist, his travels in time have given him a vast arsenal of weaponry and machinery he can utilize, including an anti-matter defense screen generator and an electromagnetic field amplifier. He also has an army of warriors to call on and a number of highly advanced robots—including his Growing Man android.

Kang's weapons come from the distant future.

Anti-graviton particle projectors in gauntlets.

STIMULOID
Kang used an android called the Growing Man to attack the Avengers and bring the team to him when Kang pitted his wits aganst the Grandmaster. At first the Wasp thought the android was a doll. Then it started to grow...

The battlesuit has its own forcefield and atmosphere.

"I PROCLAIM MYSELF KANG, THE FIRST RULER OF THE 20TH CENTURY!"

Kang once traveled back in time to prevent a bully called Morgan from slitting the 16-year-old Kang's throat. His younger self was horrified at who he would become and fled through time to the present day where he took the name Iron Lad to oppose his future self.

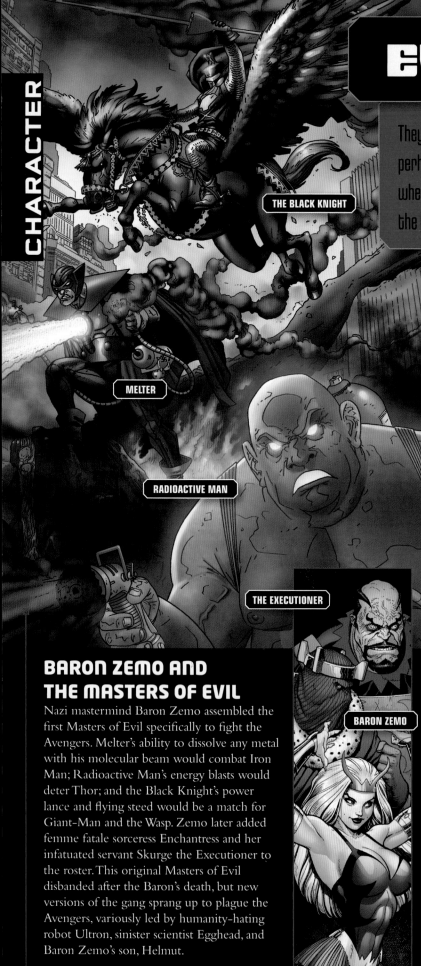

THE BLACK KNIGHT

MELTER

RADIOACTIVE MAN

THE EXECUTIONER

BARON ZEMO

ENCHANTRESS

EVIL POWERS

They prefer to remain in the shadows, pulling the strings and perhaps using other villains to fulfill their sinister stratagems. But when the likes of Dr. Doom, Magneto, and Morgan Le Fay emerge into the light, the Avengers know they have a real fight on their hands.

DR. DOOM

Combining sorcery with scientific genius, Victor Von Doom rose to power in the Balkan kingdom of Latveria. Encased in his nuclear-powered battlesuit, traversing time on his time platform, power-hungry Doom clashed with the Fantastic Four and the Avengers: his robot army attacked Avengers Mansion and held the team hostage. When it suited his purposes, however, Doom aided the team. The Dark Avengers saved Doom and rebuilt his kingdom when it was destroyed during a sorcerous battle with Morgan le Fa

BARON ZEMO AND THE MASTERS OF EVIL

Nazi mastermind Baron Zemo assembled the first Masters of Evil specifically to fight the Avengers. Melter's ability to dissolve any metal with his molecular beam would combat Iron Man; Radioactive Man's energy blasts would deter Thor; and the Black Knight's power lance and flying steed would be a match for Giant-Man and the Wasp. Zemo later added femme fatale sorceress Enchantress and her infatuated servant Skurge the Executioner to the roster. This original Masters of Evil disbanded after the Baron's death, but new versions of the gang sprang up to plague the Avengers, variously led by humanity-hating robot Ultron, sinister scientist Egghead, and Baron Zemo's son, Helmut.

MAGNETO

A mutant of awesome intellect, Magneto manipulates electromagnetic forces, controls minds, uses astral projection, and fires energy blasts from his hands. Convinced that mutants (led by himself) should rule ordinary mortals, he formed the Brotherhood of Evil Mutants. His children, Quicksilver and the Scarlet Witch, elected to join the Avengers, fueling his implacable enmity toward Earth's Mightiest.

KORVAC

The omnipotent Korvac came from a possible 31st century. His attempt to remodel the Earth to his liking brought him into conflict with the Avengers. Korvac slew many heroes, but the distress of his beloved wife led him to abandon his goal. Korvac restored the dead heroes and appeared to take his own life.

MORGAN LE FAY

The immortal sorceress from the time of King Arthur—but with designs on modern reality—has crossed the Avengers more than once. She battled Norman Osborn's Dark Avengers—until her on-off lover Dr. Doom used magic to send her back to 1,000,000 BCE.

THE SKRULLS

The Avengers clashed with the shapeshifting alien Skrulls while attempting to stop the Kree-Skrull War. Skrull agents later impersonated Super Heroes, Edwin Jarvis, and world leaders in a secret invasion of Earth. Only the genius of Reed Richards and the powers of the Avengers saved humanity from submission to Skrull rule.

SPACE PHANTOM

BLOODHAWK

THE KALUSIANS

ATTUMA

THANOS

MONOLITH

MANDARIN

A ROGUES GALLERY

The shapeshifting Space Phantom; alien threats Terminus and Thanos; underworld ruler Mole Man; cult leaders Serpent Supreme and Lion God; the Circus of Crime and Zodiac gangs; masterminds the Red Skull and Egghead; insane bird-man Bloodhawk… Villainous threats can come in all guises, and from anywhere. Battling to keep the planet safe for all, the Avengers have come to expect the totally unexpected.

TYPHON

SERPENT SUPREME

TERMINUS

GRIM REAPER

A.I.M.

THE LAVA MEN

ZODIAC

STINGER

DRAGON MAN

MR. HYDE

PYRON

THE RED SKULL

EGGHEAD

DEATHBIRD

THE ASSASSIN

CIRCUS OF CRIME

MOLE MAN

LION GOD

RED RONIN

GRAVITON

SCORPIO

TASKMASTER

BERSERKER

PILEDRIVER

45

GOVERNMENT LIAISON

Henry Peter Gyrich was the official government liaison to Earth's Mightiest Heroes. His presence foreshadowed the Superhuman Registration Act that would eventually fracture the team.

"I'M THE GOVERNMENT, MISTER... ANY MORE QUESTIONS?"

HENRY PETER GYRICH

No-nonsense National Security Council Agent Henry Peter Gyrich was assigned to investigate concerns the federal government had with America's resident super-team. On the heels of the group's headquarters-razing battle against Count Nefaria, Gyrich marched into Avengers Mansion and began making changes, threatening to revoke special privileges if the Avengers didn't institute stringent new security policies. The Avengers' access to classified government information was at stake as well as the team's ability to fly its Quinjet without air traffic restrictions. Aside from his new directives, Gyrich's innate distrust of the Avengers (and Super Heroes in general) made him more a thorn in the team's side than a bridge to better relations with the government.

Despite Gyrich's long experience with superhumans, he distrusts costumed heroes, especially those with extraterrestrial connections.

One of Gyrich's first tasks was to trim the Avengers' swollen roster to a core group of seven members chosen according to his own criteria.

RAYMOND SIKORSKI

Raymond Sikorski, a National Security Advisor and Roxxon Oil executive, succeeded Gyrich as Avengers Liaison and vowed to be much less bureaucratic. Sikorski later joined the Commission on Superhuman Activities.

Created to monitor superhuman activity in the United States, the Commission on Superhuman Activities also oversaw the superhumans who served American interests abroad. The CSA gave Julia Carpenter her powers to become the second Spider-Woman, while the department's policies would later help to define the Superhuman Registration Act.

SHIELD

Strategic Hazard Intervention Espionage Logistics Directorate

SHIELD's headquarters was in a huge mobile Helicarrier command base.

During World War II, Sgt. Nicholas Joseph Fury was known as the leader of the Howling Commandos, an elite squad of soldiers. After the war, Nick became a CIA agent, and later the Director of SHIELD. A valued friend of the Avengers, Fury was later dismissed by SHIELD and went underground, reforming the Howling Commandos and carrying out missions to protect the United States.

INCEPTION

At its inception, SHIELD stood for Supreme Headquarters, International Espionage, Law-enforcement Division—a super spy agency with a worldwide reach that worked to thwart any global or extraterrestrial threat to Earth. SHIELD initially took its marching orders from the United Nations Security Council, but it soon became too unwieldy to be managed properly. It was ultimately infiltrated and usurped by operatives of the HYDRA criminal consortium before being dismantled. The new SHIELD was formed soon after with Maria Hill as Director, and restructured so its remit focused mainly on U.S. interests. Later, Tony Stark took over, with Hill as his deputy. SHIELD technology was upgraded and morale improved, but manipulations by Iron Man's longtime foe the Mandarin led to SHIELD being mired in two international incidents, which weakened the cohesiveness of the agency just at the time of the Skrulls' Secret Invasion.

Captain America and Nick Fury are old friends and frequent allies, having first crossed paths battling Nazis during the Second World War.

SWORD

A subdivision of SHIELD, the U.N.-sanctioned Sentient World Observation and Response Department deals with counter-terrorism and monitors alien threats to world security. Special Agent Abigail Brand leads SWORD from its orbiting command center, The Peak. Other agents include Hank McCoy (Beast), Jessica Drew (Spider-Woman), and the X-Men's dragon mascot, Lockheed.

ABIGAIL BRAND

Following the Secret Invasion, Gyrich was made Co-Director of SWORD. He tried to deport several heroic aliens, and was coerced into leaving SWORD.

HAMMER

Also formed in the wake of the Skrull attacks, HAMMER was overseen by Norman Osborn to shore up America's defense network left compromised by SHIELD's failure. HAMMER gave Osborn control over the Fifty State Initiative, which he used to create the Dark Avengers. HAMMER was dissolved following the Siege of Asgard.

LOVE AND TEARS

There have been several romantic team-ups within the Avengers. Unfortunately, the pressures on two busy Super Heroes in love can often prove insurmountable.

JANET AND HANK

Janet (the Wasp) was heiress to a fortune, Hank (Ant-Man) was poor but brilliant, pushing the boundaries of science. When Hank discovered Pym Particles, which could shrink a person to the size of an ant or cause them to grow to the size of a giant, Janet enthusiastically participated in trials. They were partners in heroism, and partners in love— for a while.

Hank's scientific genius backfired when he accidentally created the rogue robot Ultron. Hank later fell victim to paranoid rages, even lashing out at his loving wife, Jan.

Hank's mental instability led to ejection from the Avengers and divorce from Janet (see pages 98-99). Despite all the hurt and anguish Hank had caused her, Janet found it very hard to say goodbye.

Years later, Jan and Hank met up again in Las Vegas and Hank proposed marriage once more. Jan turned him down, but the love, passion, and belief in each other remained. Perhaps they could come to terms with the past and forge a future together.

"You thought you'd found the strong silent hero. But I was never that strong, Jan. You know that now."

THE VISION AND THE SCARLET WITCH

Was there ever a more unlikely couple than the Vision and the Scarlet Witch (Wanda Maximoff)? One was an android, the other a passionate mutant. Yet these two opposites matched up perfectly. They married and, thanks to the Scarlet Witch's hex powers, had two children. But their domestic bliss did not last. The Vision's leadership of the Avengers ended in disaster when he tried to take control of the world's defense systems. He was dismantled and rebuilt as an emotionless, white husk. Although he would later acquire new emotional powers, his relationship with the increasingly unstable Wanda was never the same.

The kidnapping of her children brought Wanda close to breaking point. Then she discovered that her children were fragments of a demon's soul! Her emotionless husband was powerless to give her the love and support she needed and the marriage foundered.

SWORDSMAN AND MANTIS

The Avenger Mantis's turbulent relationship with Swordsman (Jacques Duquesne) began when, her mind wiped, she met him while working in a Vietnamese bar. She helped him turn his life around and they joined the Avengers together. But Mantis became infatuated with the Vision and spurned her former lover—she only realized how much she loved Swordsman when he lay dying, slain by Kang the Conqueror.

Flirtatious Mantis made the Vision blush when she gave him a kiss. Later, however, he would reject her.

HAWKEYE AND MOCKINGBIRD

Barbara "Bobbi" Morse (Mockingbird) and Clint Barton (Hawkeye) met while battling Crossfire. Clint proudly showed off his new wife to the Avengers before the couple left to set up the West Coast branch. But the relationship soon hit trouble. Mockingbird was brainwashed by Phantom Rider and forgot Clint and her past life. Recovered, she and Clint fell out when she let Phantom Rider die. Bobbi later seemingly died in Clint's arms, saving him from Mephisto. They reunited in the heroic age, but it didn't last. Despite all that fate throws at them, Bobbi and Clint remain an item.

THE AVENGERS MANSION

HISTORY

The team needed a safe and secure meeting place for strategizing and training, as well as relaxing.

Located at 980 Fifth Avenue, Manhattan, New York City, Avengers Mansion has at various times been the headquarters of the Avengers team and the base for their equipment, vehicles, and weapons. Built in 1932 by industrialist Howard Stark, the spectacular building was originally the Stark family home. When Tony Stark donated the mansion to the Avengers, the Starks' redoubtable butler, Edwin Jarvis, stayed on. The mansion has three floors above ground and three below. The first, or main, floor was sometimes opened to the public. The basement levels contained the Avengers' top-secret equipment and technology. The mansion was protected by high-tech security systems, a steel fence on the Fifth Avenue side, and a 12-foot steel-reinforced concrete wall on the other three sides. Nevertheless, over the years the mansion has been infiltrated by various Super Villains, including Kang the Conqueror and his Anachronauts, who entered via a time portal in the basement. The mansion was destroyed on two occasions, first by Baron Zemo and his Masters of Evil, after which the team relocated to Hydro-Base, a floating platform. Rebuilt on its original site, the mansion then fell victim to the Gatherers, a team of Avengers from other dimensions, mind-controlled by Proctor. The Watcher Ute, escaping Proctor's influence, presented the Avengers with an identical replacement from another reality. This mansion survived numerous attacks until reduced to rubble by a crazed Scarlet Witch. The building stayed a ruin for some time, as Stark lacked the funds to restore it.

Captain America, the Avengers' chief trainer, put many a member to the test in the mansion's state-of-the-art gym.

The delusional Scarlet Witch, believing the Avengers had taken her "children" from her, violently disassembled the team with her magic and laid waste the mansion.

EDWIN JARVIS

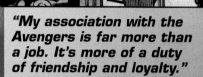

"My association with the Avengers is far more than a job. It's more of a duty of friendship and loyalty."

A former RAF pilot and war hero, the impeccable Edwin Jarvis was the Stark family butler before taking on the role of major domo when the Starks' mansion became the Avengers' base. In addition to normal housekeeping duties, Jarvis had the skills to maintain the Avengers' Quinjets. Although he had other staff to help, he was the only servant who actually lived on the premises, a fact that exposed him to peril whenever the mansion came under attack. Despite being attacked, injured, even tortured (by Kang the Conqueror), Jarvis's loyalty to the team has never wavered. He takes his role very seriously, once remarking to Spider-Man: "I have many fine qualities, sir, but jesting is not amongst them."

When forming the Mighty Avengers, Amadeus Cho and Jocasta went in search of Jarvis, realizing how useful he could be.

While on a visit to his mother in the Bronx, Jarvis used his skills as a former RAF boxing champ to take down a neighborhood bully and mugger.

"Good show, Jarvis!"

Being the Avengers' manservant is a risky business. During the Civil War, Jarvis was seriously wounded when a grudge-holding Stark ex-employee named Kenny infiltrated Avengers Tower.

MANSION CROSS SECTION

QUINJET BASE The top floor once contained a hangar and take-off and landing dock for the Avengers' Quinjet, as well as navigation equipment.

FRONT GATE Screening devices monitor all visitors to the mansion.

THE GYM This comprises a fully equipped gymnasium, an Olympic-size swimming pool, and sauna and steam room.

CRYOGENIC STORAGE Allows team members or foes to be placed in suspended animation.

MAIN ASSEMBLY ROOM If walls could talk, this room would be privy to many world-saving decisions! The Avengers' top-secret meetings were held here. The latest security devices ensure total privacy.

SECURE ROOM A virtually impregnable room to retreat to if foes penetrated the mansion's defenses.

FIRING RANGE Even Avengers need to practice! Hawkeye in particular could often be found here, devising trick arrows and perfecting his aim.

LIVING QUARTERS Avengers staying at the mansion were accommodated in its eight master bedroom suites and four guest rooms on the second floor. Jarvis's quarters were also here.

OPERATING THEATER State-of the-art medical care was available if a team member needed urgent attention.

BATTLE TRAINING Avengers honed their fighting skills in simulated battles in a reinforced room on the first basement level.

GENERATOR ROOM If a Super Villain cuts the main power supply, the mansion's independent power source on the second basement level kicks in.

COMPUTER ROOM The nerve-center. The Avengers' system was networked to the Pentagon, SHIELD, and the Fantastic Four. It contained the team's operational, crime, and forensic files.

ARSENAL CHAMBER The main store-house and testing area for Tony Stark's Iron Man armors past and present as well as weaponry and equipment.

A NEW START

In time, Tony Stark's financial fortunes recovered enough for him to restore the mansion to its former glory. With the main Avengers team now based in Avengers Tower (formerly Stark Tower), Stark sold the refurbished building to Luke Cage for one dollar, so that Cage could use the mansion as a base for his own Avengers outfit.

STARK TOWER

HISTORY

When Avengers Mansion was destroyed during the Scarlet Witch's remaking of reality (see pages 132–133), its remains were left as a memorial to one of the Avengers' darkest days. Later, the team—assembled by Captain America and Iron Man—once again benefited from the philanthropy of Tony Stark. He provided a meeting place for the Avengers in the uppermost floors of Stark Tower in midtown Manhattan. The skyscraper was soon known as "Avengers Tower," and it provided a lofty perch from which Earth's Mightiest Heroes could guard over not just the greatest city on Earth, but the entire planet. Unfortunately, however, having a high-profile (and public) address has also placed the new Avengers' headquarters in the crosshairs of major conflicts. And being so involved in global crises means it is difficult to avoid a fair amount of collateral damage...

Heimdall's Observatory atop Stark Tower is a reminder to humankind that Asgard will do anything in its power to protect Earth. Its typically Asgardian design is a relic of Asgardian power, but it cannot link to the rainbow bridge known as Bifrost.

Tony Stark intended the top three floors of Stark Tower to be his personal residence, but instead encouraged the Avengers to make the penthouse their space.

Edwin Jarvis supervised the staff at Avengers Mansion and was the team's closest confidante for years. The former pilot remains in the Avengers' employ, overseeing day-to-day operations at Stark Tower and maintaining the team's Quinjets and other aircraft.

SENTRY'S BASE

Hanging directly over Stark Tower, Sentry's base of operations appeared when he joined the team. Due to his wavering memory, it appeared and disappeared a few times before merging fully with Stark Tower. The Watchtower vanished once more upon Sentry's death at the hands of Thor.

TOWER TECH

Stark Tower comprises 93 stories and stands 1,138 feet tall, not including Heimdall's Observatory. The uppermost floor serves as the Avengers' "War Room," affording a panoramic view of Manhattan with holographic computer displays and real-time video news feeds. It also has secure communication links to SHIELD, SWORD, and the White House. The remaining two penthouse floors include living quarters for all members, as well as kitchen facilities, training rooms, and an armory. The team's various aerial vehicles—helicopters, sky-cycles, and Quinjets, are launched from rooftop hangars. Stark Tower also features a retractable dome that protects the Avengers' headquarters as needed. The tower is built from Vibranium reinforced concrete and steel to withstand anything, from a major seismic event to Super Villain attacks.

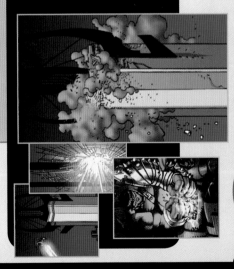

HULK SMASH!

During the events of "World War Hulk," two founding Avengers nearly toppled the tower when the Green Goliath's attempts to raze New York City brought him into violent conflict with Iron Man. Despite suffering massive damage from Hulk, Stark Tower was rebuilt and fortified.

When Norman Osborn took control of SHIELD and renamed it HAMMER, he claimed ownership of Stark Tower. Tony Stark took back the tower when Osborn was ousted from HAMMER.

LINK TO ASGARD

Following the siege and destruction of Asgard, Thor and a contingent of Norse Gods placed one of the only remaining Asgardian spires—Heimdall's Observatory—atop Stark Tower to herald a new alliance between Earth and Asgard. In the post-9/11 New York skyline, the tower stands tallest. And with Heimdall's Observatory atop it, only the most foolhardy of foes would ignore Thor's vow to protect Earth.

FEAR ITSELF

Most recently, the Avengers lost their skyscraper headquarters when Ben Grimm (the Thing) was transformed by an Asgardian hammer into Angrir, Breaker of Souls. Stark Tower was brought down when Angrir hurled his hammer through it. The tower was rebuilt once before, but Tony Stark told Captain America that this time he would not rebuild it.

"I know it sounds stupid, but I was insanely proud of this building." Tony Stark

THE QUINJET

The Quinjet's maiden flight ended in spectacular fashion when Black Panther flew it straight into Ymir, a Frost Giant who was devastating Black Panther's African kingdom Wakanda.

TEAM SHUTTLE

The Wakanda Design Group, led by brilliant scientist Black Panther, originally designed the Quinjet to transport groups of Avengers to trouble spots anywhere on the globe and beyond. The Quinjet can fly at twice the speed of sound, has vertical take-off and landing [VTOL] capability, and five "specially modified" jet engines. Quinjets can operate in Earth's atmosphere, under the sea, and in outer space. Unfortunately, they seldom return to base intact at the end of a mission. A Quinjet costs around $250 million, so repair bills must be eye-watering!

Formerly based at the Avengers Mansion, the Quinjets were relocated to the top of Stark Tower. When the U.S. Federal Aeronautical Association stopped the Avengers flying over Manhattan, the team moved the Quinjets to the Hydro-Base.

AETV-12376

ALL-PURPOSE CRAFT

The Quinjet can transport the Avengers to the furthest reaches of outer space or the darkest depths of the oceans. On a space mission, the pilot can switch to photon drive, which gives half light speed for six seconds. This enabled Iron Man and the Vision to reach in minutes an alien spacecraft orbiting the moon. The Quinjet can also switch from normal flight to submarine mode in seconds.

QUINJETTA

Would-be heroes the Great Lakes Avengers needed transport, so a Volkswagen Jetta, an ordinary auto with no flying capability, became their "Quin-jetta." At least the Quinjetta had a police scanner, so the team could find out where the Super Villain action was. It was totaled in a battle with Maelstrom.

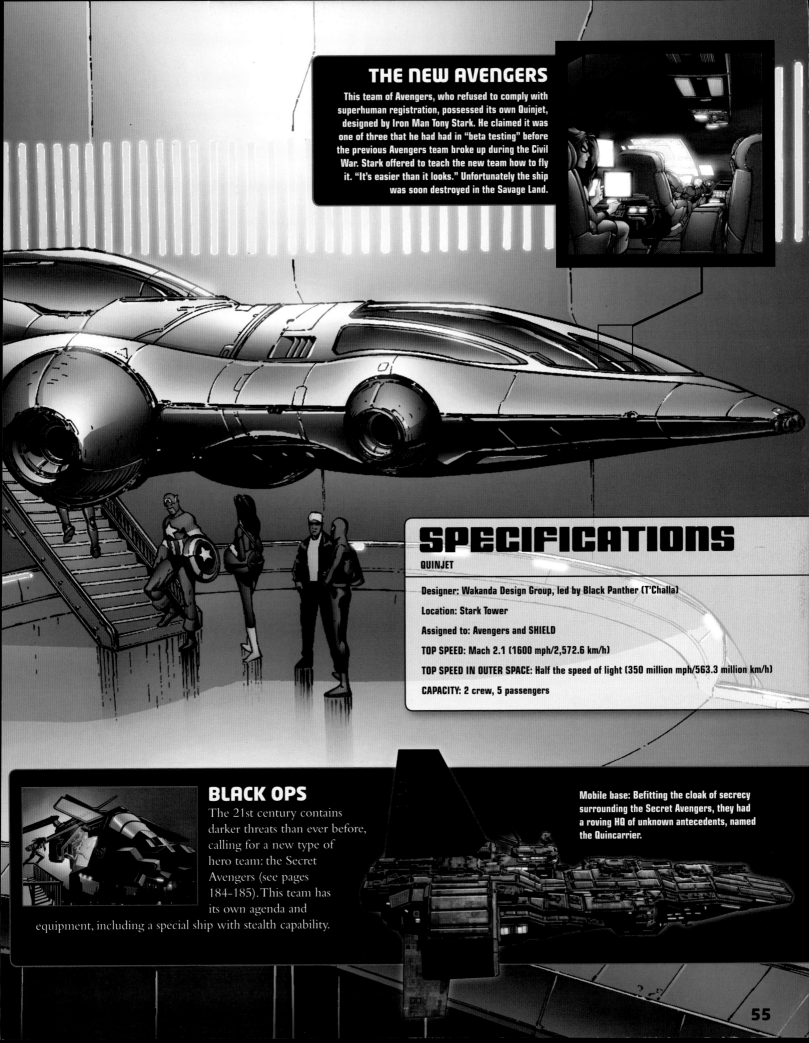

THE NEW AVENGERS

This team of Avengers, who refused to comply with superhuman registration, possessed its own Quinjet, designed by Iron Man Tony Stark. He claimed it was one of three that he had had in "beta testing" before the previous Avengers team broke up during the Civil War. Stark offered to teach the new team how to fly it. "It's easier than it looks." Unfortunately the ship was soon destroyed in the Savage Land.

SPECIFICATIONS

QUINJET

Designer: Wakanda Design Group, led by Black Panther (T'Challa)

Location: Stark Tower

Assigned to: Avengers and SHIELD

TOP SPEED: Mach 2.1 (1600 mph/2,572.6 km/h)

TOP SPEED IN OUTER SPACE: Half the speed of light (350 million mph/563.3 million km/h)

CAPACITY: 2 crew, 5 passengers

BLACK OPS

The 21st century contains darker threats than ever before, calling for a new type of hero team: the Secret Avengers (see pages 184–185). This team has its own agenda and equipment, including a special ship with stealth capability.

Mobile base: Befitting the cloak of secrecy surrounding the Secret Avengers, they had a roving HQ of unknown antecedents, named the Quincarrier.

TIMELINE

- Tricked by Loki into pursuing the Hulk, a small group of heroes including Loki's half-brother Thor, Iron Man, Ant-Man, and the Wasp fight back and decide to remain a team, calling themselves the Avengers.

- The Avengers first encounter the Space Phantom. Ant-Man becomes Giant-Man and the team sets up residence in Stark Mansion, renamed Avengers Mansion. Distrustful of his teammates, Hulk quits the team.

- Namor the Sub-Mariner allies himself with Hulk against the Avengers, a harbinger of future conflicts with the Green Goliath.

- Captain America is thawed and joins the Avengers.

- Baron Zemo forms the first Masters of Evil and pits them against the Avengers to have his revenge on Captain America.

- Iron Man is the first Avenger to face formal disciplinary action when his teammates vote to suspend his membership for one week following his failure to answer an Avengers alarm.

- The Avengers first thwart Kang the Conqueror.

- Wonder Man, a pawn of Baron Zemo, joins the Avengers and dies soon after while rebelling against his master in order to save Earth's Mightiest Heroes.

- Spider-Man is first considered for Avengers membership. Unfortunately, this Spider-Man is actually a robot created by Kang. Though the real Spider-Man helps Earth's Mightiest Heroes, he does not join the team.

- The Avengers first meet Count Nefaria.

- The original Avengers roster takes much needed leaves-of-absence. An open call for new members brings in Hawkeye, Quicksilver, and the Scarlet Witch, forming Cap's "Kooky Quartet."

- The Avengers first meet the Swordsman, a foe in his next several encounters with the team.

- Dr. Doom joins the Avengers' rogues gallery after imprisoning Earth's Mightiest Heroes in Latveria in order to lure the Fantastic Four into a trap.

- Prince Namor returns as an ally this time, working with the Avengers to thwart the Atlantean warlord Attuma.

- Giant-Man adopts a new codename (Goliath) as the Avengers battle the Collector to free the Wasp from his clutches.

- The Avengers first encounter the Living Laser, who later reforms to briefly join the team.

- When Hercules is banished from Mount Olympus for a year, the Avengers offer him a home at Avengers Mansion. He does not officially join the team until later. Because of Captain America's brief departure from the Avengers, team leader status reverts to a rotating chairperson.

- Hank Pym regains the ability to control ants and returns to the Avengers as Ant-Man.

- Captain America resigns now that Ant-Man has returned to the Avengers. Dane Whitman assumes the role of Black Knight. Magneto forces his children, the Scarlet Witch and Quicksilver to leave the Avengers and rejoin his mutant crusade.

- Hank Pym's growing ability is restored and he becomes Goliath once again.

- The Black Panther joins the Avengers on Captain America's recommendation and saves the team from the Grim Reaper, Wonder Man's brother.

- Magneto pits the X-Men against the Avengers—the first meeting of the two heroic teams.

- Ultron-5 is created by Hank Pym.

- Klaw, Whirlwind, Radioactive Man, and the Melter unite to fight the Avengers as a new incarnation of the Masters of Evil.

- Ultron-5 reveals himself to the Avengers, beginning the Living Automaton's long enmity with the team and his ongoing attempts to annihilate humanity.

- The Scarlet Centurion (Rama-Tut) sets the Avengers of an alternate universe (virtual duplicates of the team's founders) against Earth's Mightiest Heroes.

- The Avengers first meet the synthezoid Vision, who later joins the team.

- Exposure to an untested gas induces schizophrenia in Hank Pym, who adopts the identity of Yellowjacket. He forces the Wasp to marry him, not realizing that she knows he is really Hank Pym. The shock of seeing the Wasp in jeopardy during the wedding reception restores Hank's memory.

- The Avengers travel to Wakanda, home of the Black Panther, and battle Man-Ape for the first time.

- Hawkeye uses Hank Pym's growth serum to become a new Goliath.

- The head of Ultron-5 perched atop a rocket-propelled body made from a molecularly rearranged Adamantium cylinder becomes Ultron-6.

- The Avengers first battle the Squadron Sinister.

- The Avengers first face the international crime cartel the Zodiac.

- Quicksilver and the Scarlet Witch return to the Avengers in time for the team to thwart Arkon for the first time.

- The Grim Reaper forms his Lethal Legion which includes Avengers adversaries Power Man, Living Laser, Man-Ape, and the Swordsman.

- The Wasp returns home to the mansion to find the team's headquarters briefly taken over by a feminist super-team called the Liberators, with members including Medusa of the Inhumans, Black Widow, Valkyrie, and the Scarlet Witch.

- The Black Panther leaves the Avengers to return to Wakanda.

- Captain Marvel frees himself from the Negative Zone and the Avengers and Rick Jones race to decontaminate Marvel at Cape Canaveral, where they encounter a Kree Sentry. The Kree-Skrull War begins with Ronan the Accuser plotting the overthrow of the Supreme Intelligence in order to rule the Kree Empire.

- Yellowjacket and the Wasp resign from the Avengers. The Pyms rejoin and leave the team at various times during their marriage.

- The Avengers are accused of collaborating with the Kree by the Alien Activities Commission. The Avengers briefly disband believing they were irresponsible in aiding Captain Marvel.

• Hank Pym becomes Ant-Man once again.

• Rick Jones uses the near-omnipotent powers granted by the Omni-Wave to immobilize the warring Kree and Skrulls, ending the war and merges with Captain Marvel.

• The Avengers encounter the mutant-hunting robot Sentinels, one of which reveals the true age of the Vision's synthezoid body and hints at a previous "life" for the android Avenger.

• After the longest membership of any Avenger, Hawkeye resigns.

• After a battle with Magneto, Captain America offers membership to Daredevil and Black Widow. The Man Without Fear declines, but the former Soviet spy accepts, albeit briefly.

• When the public learns of the Vision and the Scarlet Witch's romance, an anti-android suicide bomber nearly destroys the Vision.

• The Swordsman joins the Avengers, while Mantis is made a provisional member of the team.

• Following a pitched battle with the Zodiac, the criminal cartel's Libra reveals that he is Mantis' father.

• The Avengers first encounter the alien tyrant Thanos, who will later possess the fabled Infinity Gauntlet.

• At Quicksilver's marriage to the Inhumans' Crystal, Earth's Mightiest Heroes grapple with the robot Omega, soon revealed to be Ultron-7 in disguise!

• During a time-spanning battle with Kang, the Swordsman gives his life to save Mantis.

• The Swordsman is resurrected by the Cotati as the "Celestial Madonna" adventure begins. Upon its conclusion, Vision weds the Scarlet Witch. And Mantis weds the Swordsman, with Immortus officiating at the double-wedding.

• Yellowjacket and the Wasp rejoin the Avengers. Beast and Moondragon join the team as provisional members.

• After another historic adventure to thwart Kang (this time in 1873), the Avengers return to their own time with the Two-Gun Kid in tow. Hawkeye rejoins to help save the time-lost team.

• Hellcat joins the Avengers.

• A roster restructuring leads to a new team of full-time Avengers: Captain America, the Wasp, Iron Man, Beast, the Scarlet Witch, and the Vision. Meanwhile, Thor, Hawkeye, Moondragon, Hellcat, and Yellowjacket become reserve members-on-call.

• Wonder Man is resurrected as a zombie by the Black Talon.

• A returned Wonder Man teams up with the Avengers once more, leading to his later membership with the team he was created to destroy.

• Ultron-8 attacks when a memory-addled Hank Pym assumes his Ant-Man identity once more. Ultron-8 kidnaps the Wasp to use her psyche as a template for his "bride," Jocasta.

• National Security Council Agent Henry Peter Gyrich begins his liaison relationship with the Avengers.

• Count Nefaria is imbued with all the powers of the Lethal Legion.

• Thanos assembles the six Soul Gems, which he will later use to form the Infinity Gauntlet, as the Avengers join forces with Adam Warlock and Captain Marvel to defeat the tyrant of Titan.

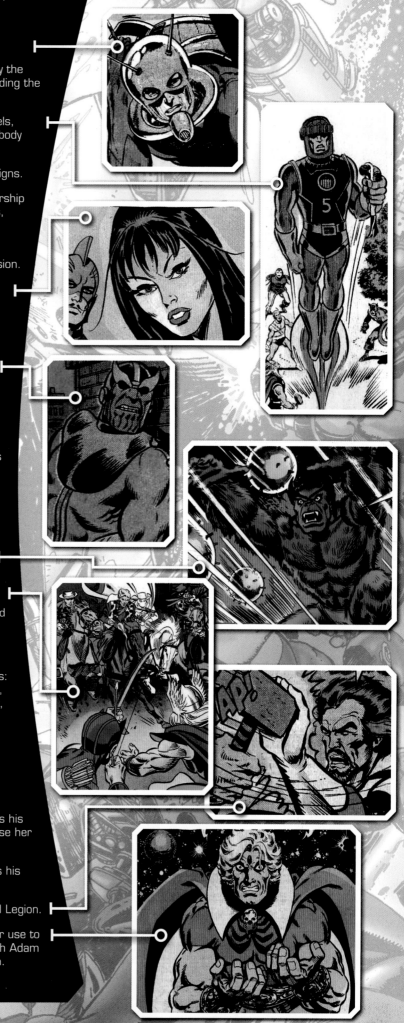

• The Avengers first encounter Michael Korvac and join forces with the Guardians of the Galaxy.

• The Avengers continue to battle Korvac on one front and the Collector on another. Captain Marvel and the Whizzer are listed as honorary members of the team. Gyrich calls a meeting of all 22 presently active Avengers, limiting the team to a core roster. The Falcon is selected by Gyrich and a government mandate to add a minority member to Earth's Mightiest Heroes.

• Wonder Man is awarded full membership status.

• Ms. Marvel joins the Avengers.

• During the "Knights of Wundagore" adventure, Quicksilver and the Scarlet Witch learn their true origins, including the truth that Magneto is their father.

• Wonder Man rejoins the Avengers as Falcon departs the team.

• Jocasta is made a provisional member.

• Ultron attacks the Avengers once again, and Earth's Mightiest Heroes defeat him this time by encasing the Adamantium android in… Adamantium.

• Perhaps a harbinger of events to come, a Skrull masquerades as Jarvis and poisons Beast's girlfriend, Vera Cantor.

• Ms. Marvel's powers and memory are stolen by the mutant Rogue, effectively ending her Super Hero career (and Avengers membership) for a brief time.

• Tigra joins the Avengers. Jocasta is also finally made an Avenger, but, believing herself unloved and unaware of the vote, departs Earth's Mightiest Heroes.

• Yellowjacket is court-martialed by the Avengers for endangering civilians and departs the team after the disciplinary hearing. Later, after apparently aiding Egghead against the team, he is imprisoned.

• Captain Marvel dies of cancer caused by exposure to a nerve toxin years earlier.

• During a new membership drive following Tigra's resignation and Yellowjacket's expulsion, Hawkeye rejoins the team, which also adds She-Hulk as a member.

• Following "The Trial of Yellowjacket," Hank Pym is exonerated but decides to hang up his Yellowjacket costume for good, leaving superheroics behind (for now). Monica Rambeau (Captain Marvel) is made a provisional member before becoming a full Avenger in just a short time.

• Jocasta is destroyed when she attempts to overload Ultron's weaponry in order to destroy him.

• Starfox joins the Avengers as a member-in-training.

• After turning down previous invitations to join, Spider-Man breaks into Avengers Mansion, ready to be a member. But he is denied membership because the team's roster is full.

• The Avengers appear on *Late Night With David Lettermen*, battling villain Fabian Stankowicz as the show airs live.

• Appointed new chairman of the Avengers, the Vision obtains permission from its government liaisons to form the West Coast Avengers with Hawkeye as the expansion team's leader. Starfox gains full membership privileges.

- Mockingbird and War Machine join the West Coast Avengers.

- The Vision proposes a midwestern branch of the Avengers, but nothing comes of it. The "Great Lakes Avengers" that appear later are unsanctioned.

- Namor the Sub-Mariner joins the Avengers.

- A corrupted Moondragon is destroyed when she is turned to ash.

- The mystic Dr. Druid joins the team.

- Namor uses the Black Knight's Ebony Blade to kill his wife and Avengers teammate Marrina in her monstrous Leviathan form.

- The Vision is dismantled and reassembled by the U.S. government without any knowledge of his past.

- Moondragon is resurrected on Titan in a new body.

- Mantis is grown a new body by the Cotati.

- Nebula joins the Avengers.

- She-Hulk, Black Knight, Thor, and Dr. Druid quit the Avengers, leaving Jarvis to shut down the Hydro-Base.

- The Captain (Steve Rogers) is sole member of the East Coast-based Avengers.

- Rita DeMara (Yellowjacket II) joins the team.

- The Captain recruits Mr. Fantastic, the Invisible Woman, Thor, and Gilgamesh to fill the ranks of the depleted Avengers.

- Suffering her first bout of insanity, the Scarlet Witch kills Wonder Man in space, but soon after alters reality to resurrect him.

- As Captain America once again, Steve Rogers gathers all the Avengers into a single team based on Avengers Island.

- Doorman, Dinah Soar, Mr. Immortal, Big Bertha, and Flatman band together to form the Great Lakes Avengers.

- Gilgamesh departs the Avengers.

- Wendell Vaughn (Quasar) joins the team.

- Sersi becomes a member of Earth's Mightiest Heroes.

- Spider-Man finally joins the Avengers, but asks that his membership be rescinded and departs after just a few adventures.

- Stingray joins the Avengers.

- Rage and Sandman are inducted as probationary members, but neither become full-fledged Avengers.

- Crystal joins the Avengers.

- Thunderstrike is added to the roster of Earth's Mightiest Heroes.

- The Avengers first encounter Proctor and the Gatherers.

- Mockingbird is killed by Mephisto as she saves her husband Hawkeye from incineration by Mephisto.

- Magdalene is granted honorary membership in the Avengers.

- Earth's Mightiest Heroes meet Deathcry, beginning her association and honorary membership with the team.

- Hellcat commits suicide with the help of Deathurge.

- The Black Knight learns that Proctor is actually an alternate reality doppelganger of himself.

- Wonder Man is destroyed by a Kree bomb.

- The Space Phantoms return, dispatched by Immortus to bedevil the Avengers. Yellowjacket II is slain.

- Masque, a clone of Madame Masque, joins the team.

- The Avengers battle Onslaught and many are killed. The surviving heroes find themselves reborn in a pocket universe created by Franklin Richards.

- Earth's Mightiest Heroes return to their own world and reestablish the Avengers in time to battle Morgan Le Fay, who remakes reality to her own dark designs.

- The Scarlet Witch restores Wonder Man to life.

- Justice and Firestar are inducted as Avengers reservists, later gaining full membership.

- The Avengers suffer massive collateral damage at the hands of Whirlwind, leading to a much-needed, more streamlined team.

- Triathlon joins the team, later calling himself 3-D Man.

- Silverclaw becomes an Avenger.

- Jack of Hearts joins Earth's Mightiest Heroes.

- Lionheart is added to the Avengers roster.

- Following a series of attacks by the Scarlet Witch, the Avengers officially disband. Jack of Hearts (dispatched by the Scarlet Witch) destroys Avengers Mansion. The Vision is torn to synthezoid shreds by She-Hulk. Hawkeye perishes combating a Kree warship.

- A massive Super Villain prison break from the Raft unites several former teammates and others to form a new Avengers lineup.

- Becoming further mentally unhinged, the Scarlet Witch remakes reality with mutants as the ruling majority. The Avengers unite to restore the world to normal, but at a cost to mutants.

- The Vision is rebuilt and reactivated.

- The Superhuman Registration Act is passed, sparking Civil War. Captain America dies in defense of heroes' rights.

- Iron Man becomes Director of SHIELD. His 50-State Initiative begins a government-sponsored training program for sanctioned Super Hero teams across the U.S. Iron Man picks a team of Mighty Avengers.

- Captain America is apparently assassinated. Bucky Barnes takes over the role of Cap for a brief time.

- Hulk returns from exile in space vowing vengeance on the Illuminati, waging war on all Super Heroes, including his former Avengers teammates.

- The Skrulls' Secret Invasion of Earth escalates into all-out war.

- After killing the Skrull Queen, Norman Osborn replaces Tony Stark as Director of SHIELD (renamed HAMMER) and uses stolen Iron Man armor to become the Iron Patriot, leader of a group of Dark Avengers.

- The Avengers reform with a brand new lineup and the new Heroic Age begins. The new team's headquarters is at Stark Tower.

- The Young Avengers team forms, a team of superpowered fanboys.

- The Avengers Academy opens.

the 1960s

was replaced by one including the Scarlet Witch and Quicksilver—two reformed Super Villains—in issue 16. Under the guidance of writer Stan Lee (and later Roy Thomas) with Marvel maestros Jack Kirby, Don Heck, and John Buscema handling the art, the first decade of *The Avengers* introduced heroes and villains that would soon become mainstays of the Marvel Universe. When the Black Panther joined the team (in *Avengers #52*), Marvel also showed they were paying attention to the changing world around them and throwing their full-support behind the fight for equal rights taking place across the United States.

OVERLEAF

The second Avengers annual (1968) had the Avengers meeting their original lineup courtesy of the Scarlet Centurion. It was a time-traveling epic that showed a parallel world where the Avengers had become Earth's Mightiest Dictators...

1960S
Adventures

Captain America wasn't one of the original Avengers, but gained the status of founding member after Hulk left.

AVENGERS ASSEMBLE!

The Avengers had a dramatic first decade. They lost founding member Hulk after only two adventures, Hulk quitting the team when he realized how much his fellow Avengers distrusted him. His place was soon filled by Captain America when the hero's frozen body was found. Cap's membership helped the Avengers gain A-1 security clearance from the government. Cap's old nemesis Baron Zemo soon returned, backed by the Masters of Evil. Their villainy was followed by the time-traveling menaces of Kang and Immortus and the machinations of Mandarin and the Swordsman.

The team also prevented Attuma from conquering the surface world and ended the menace of the Soviet Union's answer to Captain America— the Red Guardian.

The time-traveling Kang soon became a sworn enemy of the Avengers after suffering defeat at their hands.

Rick Jones

Rick Jones was at the heart of the Avengers. He was a close friend of Cap, and briefly assumed the role of his sidekick Bucky. Rick also helped to free Captain Marvel from the Negative Zone by using the Nega-bands to swap places with the legendary hero.

Rick was a member of the Teen Brigade and it was their radio signal, requesting help from the Fantastic Four to find Hulk, that inadvertently led to the formation of the Avengers.

This is the coolest! First Thor, then Iron Man, and now Ant-Man and the Wasp! It's more than we dared hope for!
Rick Jones

After Hulk quit the Avengers, he formed an uneasy alliance with the Sub-Mariner against his old teammates. The duo came close to defeating the Avengers until Hulk transformed back into Banner and was forced to flee.

In the years after their formation, the Avengers fought alongside most of their fellow heroes at various times. Often a misunderstanding (or manipulation by a Super Villain) would lead to hero fighting hero before teaming up against a common enemy...

The first times Spidey met the Avengers, things didn't go well. The Webslinger irritated Iron Man when the Golden Avenger asked him for help. Months later, Kang sent a robot disguised as Spider-Man to attack the team. It took the real-life Spider-Man to defeat his robotic duplicate.

With Hulk on another rampage, the Avengers teamed up with the Fantastic Four for the first time in an attempt to stop him. At first, the heroes got in each other's way before Hulk fell into the river and changed back to Banner.

When the X-Men's Angel came to the Avengers for help, the heroes soon found themselves fighting the mutant's teammates, victims of Magneto's hypno-ray. The Avengers had a plan and soon had Magneto running for his life.

LATE 60S

The last few years of the decade saw a host of new members join the Avengers including the new Black Knight, Hercules, the Black Panther, and the Vision. Ant-Man (Hank Pym) went through mental trauma and became the more adventurous Yellowjacket. The hero married Janet Van Dyne (the Wasp), although the Circus of Crime gatecrashed the wedding. One of Hank's inventions, the robotic Ultron, rapidly evolved to become one of the

Dane Whitman was the nephew of the evil Black Knight. He pretended to be bad to uncover the Masters of Evil's latest scheme.

Avengers' deadliest enemies. As the decade ended, the team found itself fighting the Squadron Sinister, a team of villains created by the cosmically powered Grandmaster to best the heroes in combat.

Heroes turned out in force for the wedding of Yellowjacket and the Wasp. When the Circus of Crime attacked, Yellowjacket revealed his true identity—Hank Pym!

Ultron was created by Hank Pym and programmed with Pym's own brain patterns. Ultron soon became one of the greatest threats the Avengers ever faced. Each time Ultron returned, he had upgraded himself to become even deadlier.

THE AVENGERS
Vol.1 #52

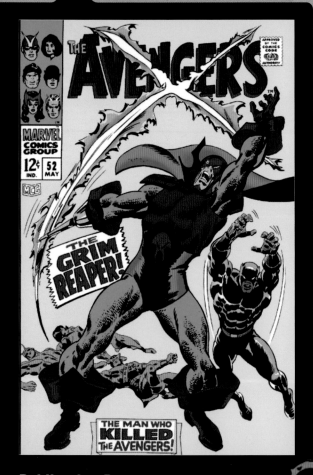

> *"What in the name of the timeless jungle which spawned me—? It's... unbelievable! The Avengers... DEAD!"*
> **Black Panther**

Main Characters: Hawkeye; Goliath; the Wasp; Black Panther (T'Challa)

Main Supporting Characters: SHIELD Agent Jasper Sitwell; Natasha Romanova

Main Locations: New York City; Avengers Mansion

Publication Date
May 1968

Editor in Chief
Stan Lee

Cover Artist
John Buscema

Writer
Roy Thomas

Penciler
John Buscema

Inker
Vince Coletta

Colorist
Uncredited

BACKGROUND

New members joined and heroes of the old guard frequently resigned throughout the history of the Avengers. If anything, the rotating roster added diversity of powers and perspective to Earth's Mightiest Heroes. But none so much as in this milestone issue, which is notable because it featured the first Super Hero of color to become an Avenger. While Marvel's premier Super Hero team had already broken down the gender barrier, this forward-thinking tale from the Avengers annals, "Death Calls For the Arch-Heroes," was released at the height of the Civil Rights struggle in the U.S. Black Panther, created by Stan Lee and Jack Kirby in 1966, prior to the founding of the Black Panther Party, was invited to join the team by none other than Captain America himself. And not a moment too soon for Hawkeye, Goliath, and the Wasp—three Super Heroes at death's door!

The Story

When Captain America asked the Black Panther to join the ranks as his replacement, a grim discovery in the Avengers Mansion meant he instantly regretted his decision. Would the Black Panther be able to prove his worth and join the team?

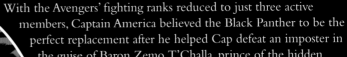

With the Avengers' fighting ranks reduced to just three active members, Captain America believed the Black Panther to be the perfect replacement after he helped Cap defeat an imposter in the guise of Baron Zemo. T'Challa, prince of the hidden African nation Wakanda, accepted Cap's invitation, entering Avengers Mansion stealthily and with heightened senses tingling upon discovering no outward signs of life **(1)**. Since he had yet to become an official member of Earth's Mightiest Heroes, the headquarters' automated security protocols—designed by Tony Stark himself—identified the Panther as an intruder, engaging the Wakandan hero in robotic game of cat-and-mouse, trapping him within an unbreakable tube **(2)**!

The Panther defeated numerous traps, winding his way to the secure center of the mansion. To his horror, the Panther found the seemingly lifeless bodies of the three full-time Avengers; Hawkeye, Goliath, and the Wasp **(3)**! While he attempted in vain to revive the dead trio, the Panther was discovered by SHIELD Agent Jasper Sitwell, an Avengers liaison who accused T'Challa of murdering Earth's Mightiest Heroes **(4)**. Held at gunpoint by Agent Sitwell until the police arrived, the Black Panther allowed himself to be arrested and booked on suspicion of hero homicide! In no time, the news spread throughout New York City and to the eyes and ears of former Avengers like Captain America and Thor, each stunned at the Panther's apparent betrayal **(5)**.

Escaping police custody to clear his good name, the Panther returned to Avengers Mansion and uncovered the true culprit, a gloating Grim Reaper! With his terrible scythe, the Grim Reaper cut down the Avengers within their own headquarters, motivated by revenge for the death of his brother Simon Williams, a.k.a. Wonder Man **(6)**. A pawn of the real Baron Zemo, the ionic-energy-fueled Wonder Man sacrificed his own life rather than fulfill his directive to destroy the Avengers **(7)**.

In a pitched battle with the Grim Reaper **(8)**, the Panther goaded the villain into revealing that he had not killed the Avengers, but had in fact rendered them paralyzed with their respective vital signs slowed to a virtual standstill. When the Grim Reaper accidentally fell upon his own terrible blade **(9)**, the Panther had no choice but to leave the wounded villain and race to the hospital where he revived the Avengers with the Grim Reaper's scythe **(10)**. Though the Grim Reaper survived and somehow escaped, the grateful heroes welcomed the Panther as the newest Avenger **(11)**!

> *"Today you have gained a new ally... For now the Panther is truly an Avenger!"*
>
> T'Challa, the Black Panther

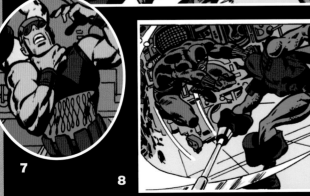

THE VISION

CHARACTER

When evil robot Ultron created a synthezoid to be his servant, it did not bode well for the Avengers—or humanity. After the Avengers unlocked the Vision's human emotions, he became their teammate.

The Vision first appeared to the Wasp before being convinced to turn on Ultron.

The Mysterious Synthezoid

The Wasp was the first Avenger to encounter the artificial human when he tried to murder her. She recounted seeing "a vision of evil," and the synthezoid gained a name. The Vision, sent by Ultron-5, was on a mission to kill the Avengers. The robot had coerced Professor T. Horton (creator of Human Torch) to help create the Vision. (The Avengers later learned that the timelord Immortus masterminded the Vision's creation.) The synthezoid was programmed with the brain patterns and emotions of villain-turned-hero Wonder Man.

The Vision unwittingly led the Avengers into a trap, but defeated Ultron and became a member of the Avengers "family." He fell in love with and wed the Scarlet Witch (fulfilling Immortus' plan to stop the Scarlet Witch having children and threatening the cosmic power balance). The Vision rose to become the Avengers' chairman but overreached his power and was disassembled by the government. He was rebuilt by Hank Pym, but without emotions, and his marriage to the unstable Scarlet Witch broke up. Her attempt to remake reality to recreate her "children" brought about the Vision's death. The Vision's programming lived on in Iron Lad's armor, until Tony Stark rebuilt him.

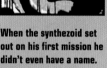

When the synthezoid set out on his first mission he didn't even have a name.

Becoming a member of the Avengers brought a tear to the Vision's eye.

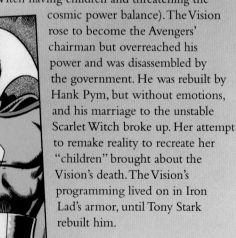

The usually calm and unemotional Vision and the troubled Scarlet Witch was a case of opposites attracting.

The Scarlet Witch discovered that the U.S. government had kidnapped and disassembled her synthezoid husband.

Hank Pym rebuilt the Vision as a chalk-white emotionless being, much to the Scarlet Witch's dismay. It took a long time for the Vision to regain his emotions and original appearance.

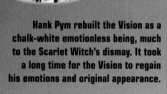

The jewel in the Vision's brow was not for show—it fired flashing blasts of solar energy.

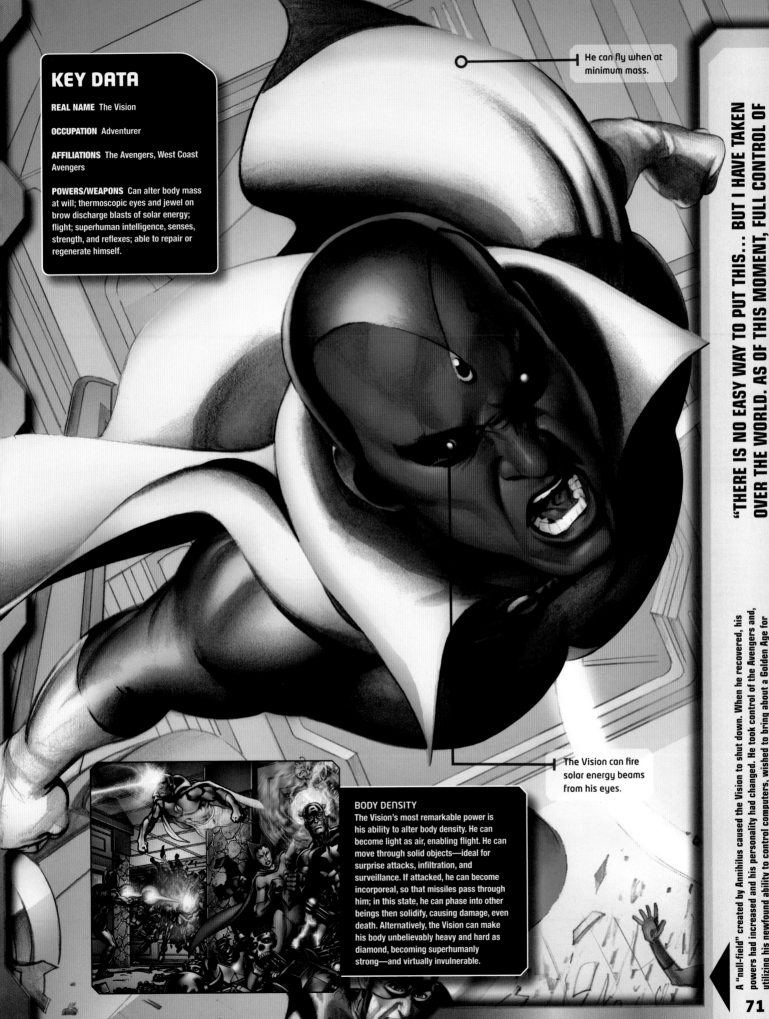

KEY DATA

REAL NAME The Vision

OCCUPATION Adventurer

AFFILIATIONS The Avengers, West Coast Avengers

POWERS/WEAPONS Can alter body mass at will; thermoscopic eyes and jewel on brow discharge blasts of solar energy; flight; superhuman intelligence, senses, strength, and reflexes; able to repair or regenerate himself.

He can fly when at minimum mass.

"THERE IS NO EASY WAY TO PUT THIS… BUT I HAVE TAKEN OVER THE WORLD. AS OF THIS MOMENT, FULL CONTROL OF THE EARTH'S WEAPONS SYSTEMS IS MINE."

The Vision can fire solar energy beams from his eyes.

BODY DENSITY

The Vision's most remarkable power is his ability to alter body density. He can become light as air, enabling flight. He can move through solid objects—ideal for surprise attacks, infiltration, and surveillance. If attacked, he can become incorporeal, so that missiles pass through him; in this state, he can phase into other beings then solidify, causing damage, even death. Alternatively, the Vision can make his body unbelievably heavy and hard as diamond, becoming superhumanly strong—and virtually invulnerable.

A "null-field" created by Annihilus caused the Vision to shut down. When he recovered, his powers had increased and his personality had changed. He took control of the Avengers and, utilizing his newfound ability to control computers, wished to bring about a Golden Age for humanity. The U.S. government was not prepared to let the Vision's vision become reality.

71

Gloves conceal metal-melting retractable claws and energy daggers.

Costume utilizes cloaking and camouflage technology to appear as civilian clothes when necessary.

The Black Panther's greatest foe was once one of his closest friends. During his first adventure with the Avengers, T'Challa's rule was challenged by M'Baku, a jealous Wakanda warrior who later revived the outlawed White Gorilla cult. M'Baku had killed one of the sacred apes, consumed its flesh, and bathed in its blood to gain superhuman powers. As the Man-Ape, M'Baku wore the hide of the white gorilla and regularly attempted to take over Wakanda despite repeated defeats by the Black Panther and the Avengers.

Vibranium pads on boot soles enable ninja-like stealth for climbing, running across water, and to ensure the Black Panther always lands on his feet!

After battling Iron Man, Dane's mortally wounded Uncle Nathan made his nephew swear to only wield the Ebony Blade for good.

THE BLACK KNIGHT

Dane Whitman is a direct descendant of Sir Percy of Scandia, one of the Arthurian Knights of the Round Table and guiding spirit to Whitman. Wielder of the enchanted Ebony Blade, Dane inherited the sword from his uncle, Nathan Garrett, the first Black Knight and a member of the Masters of Evil. On his deathbed, a repentant Garrett willed the Ebony Blade to Dane and entrusted him to take on the mantle of the Black Knight, this time fighting on the side of justice. The Black Knight proved himself to the Avengers and joined the team. Recently, he joined the UK's MI-13.

BLACK PANTHER

T'Challa (the Black Panther) is ruler of a tiny African nation called Wakanda, principal source of the world's supply of Vibranium, the energy-absorbing metal used to forge Captain America's shield. As a child, T'Challa became king after his father was murdered by the sound-wielding Super Villain Klaw. After a formal education in Europe and America, T'Challa assumed the Wakandan throne and accepted the ceremonial garb of the Black Panther, defender of Wakanda and its Vibranium riches. The Black Panther journeyed to America soon after to decide whether or not the country's Super Heroes were a threat to Wakanda. After helping Captain America defeat an imposter masquerading as Baron Zemo, T'Challa was invited to join Earth's Mightiest Heroes and he remains an Avenger. T'Challa is currently married to the X-Men's weather-manipulating mutant Storm.

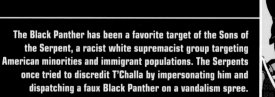

The Black Panther has been a favorite target of the Sons of the Serpent, a racist white supremacist group targeting American minorities and immigrant populations. The Serpents once tried to discredit T'Challa by impersonating him and dispatching a faux Black Panther on a vandalism spree.

Hercules and fellow Avenger, rival god, and half-brother Ares are bitter foes. Ares once allied with his mother Hera (Hercules' stepmother) who made Hercules fall in love with an illusory woman. Hercules was heartbroken when he discovered his love was not real.

HERCULES

Son of Zeus, king of the Olympian gods, and a mortal woman, Hercules is a brash demigod possessing extraordinary strength which he used to complete the fabled Twelve Labors to win immortality and a place of honor on Mount Olympus. Hercules joined the Avengers in time to help them defeat the Super-Adaptoid when the robotic rogue attacked a celebration honoring Earth's Mightiest Heroes in New York City's Central Park. Hercules was, for a time, one of the Mighty Avengers and is a close friend of Amadeus Cho.

Hercules wields a golden mace every bit as indestructible as Thor's hammer. Brazen and bold beyond measure, Hercules often greets his Avenging teammates with a punch in the face!

1960s NEW MEMBERS

The team added new rising superstars from across the Marvel Universe. These included an African king, a Olympian demigod, a mole planted by one of their worst foes, and a direct descendant from King Arthur's Round Table!

Baron Zemo bombarded Simon with ionic radiation that increased his strength, speed, and stamina. Unfortunately, Wonder Man regularly required an antidote in order to survive this treatment.

WONDER MAN

Simon Williams is the brother of the Grim Reaper. Jailed for embezzlement, he was freed by Baron Zemo, who turned him into Wonder Man, a mole meant to infiltrate the Avengers and destroy them by luring them into Zemo's deathtrap. Instead, Wonder Man turned on his creator and apparently died saving the Avengers. After being resurrected, he was offered membership as a reward for his previous sacrifice. He served with both the regular team and the short-lived West Coast Avengers.

Following his sacrifice, Wonder Man fell into a coma-like stasis during which time his body became pure ionic energy. He has since "died" many times over, each time reforming himself from his dissipated ionic energy.

the **1970s**

By the 1970s, the Avengers was firmly established as one of world's greatest super-teams. The decade also saw a huge explansion of the Marvel Universe—with the Avengers at the forefront of the action!

It was a decade that saw the further improvement of equal rights, the end of the Vietnam War, and an American President resign from office following the Watergate scandal. Creatively, the decade started with the last remaining embers of 60s flowerpower and ended with the power of punk and the rise of electronica in music. *The Avengers* produced some of its strongest sagas—from the Kree-Skrull War to the Avengers-Defenders War. The social change of the times was reflected in the creation of Valkyrie (not to mention her Lady Liberators) and the rise in prominence of the Wasp, while the introduction of Special Agent Henry Gyrich reflected the post-Watergate distrust of government. The decade also saw the lineup of the Avengers go through major changes with the Beast and Jocasta joining the team. The book was in the hands of Marvel's best creators—including such talented writers as Roy Thomas, Steve Englehart, and Gerry Conway. Artistic legends George Pérez and John Byrne burst on to the scene.

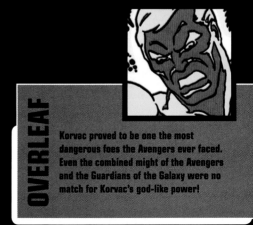

OVERLEAF

Korvac proved to be one the most dangerous foes the Avengers ever faced. Even the combined might of the Avengers and the Guardians of the Galaxy were no match for Korvac's god-like power!

CHARACTER

BLACK WIDOW

Natalia "Natasha" Romanova was a former Russian spy tasked with stealing secrets from Stark Industries. Hawkeye persuaded her to turn her back on that life and she began to work with SHIELD and the Avengers. She has heightened athletic prowess and retains her youth thanks to a Soviet variation on the Super Soldier Serum. She is armed with two bracelets; one launches a retractable "widow's line," the other fires a "widow's bite."

HELLCAT

Patricia "Patsy" Walker Hellstrom's lifelong dreams of becoming a Super Hero were fulfilled when she accompanied the Avengers on a mission and discovered the original cat costume worn by Greer Nelson (a.k.a. Tigra). Later, Patsy learned that she possessed latent psionic powers. Hellcat's catsuit enhances her strength, speed, and agility, while her natural "demon sight" allows her to sense and react to mystical phenomena.

MS. MARVEL

U.S. Air Force officer Carol Danvers first gained superpowers after exposure to unknown radiation during a battle between Captain Marvel and a Kree rival altered Carol's genetic structure and endowed her with powers similar to Marvel. Like her namesake, Carol can fly, has superstrength and stamina, and can project powerful energy blasts. She joined the Avengers after helping them to defeat the villain Ultron.

MOONDRAGON

Orphaned as a toddler when her parents were murdered by the alien conqueror Thanos, Earthling Heather Douglas was raised on Saturn's moon Titan by the genetically enhanced race known as the Eternals. On Titan, Moondragon became a highly skilled martial artist, and mastered formidable telepathic and telekinetic powers. She helped the Avengers during their first confrontation with Thanos before joining the team. She was an Avenger for only a short time.

1970s NEW MEMBERS

During the Avengers' second decade of existence, membership grew to include a greater diversity of superpowers with new and rising stars from all corners of the Marvel Universe joining Earth's Mightiest Heroes as the team faced some of its most epic space-faring sagas, as well as a host of new terrestrial threats from foes both old and new!

WONDER MAN

Like many Avengers members, Wonder Man started out as a villain. Baron Zemo gave Simon Williams superpowers in order to make the ionic-energized Wonder Man into an Avengers mole. But instead of betraying the team, Wonder Man turned on his creator and sacrificed his own life in the process. Since a being of ionic energy cannot ever truly die, Wonder Man has returned again and again to serve the Avengers in its many incarnations as a loyal and trusted member.

FALCON

Former criminal Sam Wilson was granted a telepathic link with his pet falcon Redwing by the Red Skull, who intended Wilson to befriend and later betray Captain America. Wilson overcame the Skull's brainwashing and became Cap's partner as the high-flying Falcon! A skilled fighter, the Falcon later used his jet-propelled wings to soar to new heights as an Avenger during a push to add more minority members to the team.

MANTIS

A human/plant hybrid raised in Vietnam by Kree aliens, Mantis possessed telepathic abilities that enabled her to communicate with any flora. Mantis, a martial arts adept, can also create new bodies out of plant matter, thus enabling her to traverse across space via host plant bodies. After joining the Avengers, Mantis learned that she was the "Celestial Madonna," destined to give birth to a son who would bring peace to the universe.

WHIZZER

Like Captain America, Robert Frank battled villainy during World War II, using his superspeed (the result of an injection of mongoose blood) to run

rings around the Nazis as the Whizzer. Frank came out of retirement to join the Avengers, serving alongside a new generation of Super Heroes until he was felled by a fatal heart attack.

TWO-GUN KID

Matt Hawk (born Matthew Leibowicz) was an Old West crime fighter known more familiarly as the Two-Gun Kid. The Kid met the Avengers when they

traveled to the past in pursuit of Kang, and later went back to his future to saddle up with Earth's Mightiest Heroes for a brief time. He returned to his own era after becoming homesick.

SWORDSMAN

Jacques Duquesne gained infamy as a Super Villain before reforming and using his energized blade for good. He was accepted into the Avengers

despite Hawkeye having serious doubts, but later revealed himself to be an agent of the Mandarin, Iron Man's archenemy. In the end he switched sides, and betrayed the Mandarin to save the Avengers.

BEAST

As one of the X-Men, Henry "Hank" McCoy used his superhuman agility to defend other mutants. Later, brilliant biochemist McCoy isolated a formula

that triggered mutations. Testing his concoction on himself, McCoy mutated further into a furry blue Beast. He joined the Avengers soon after, sharing scientific duties with Hank Pym.

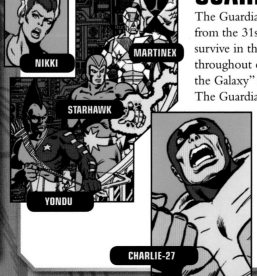

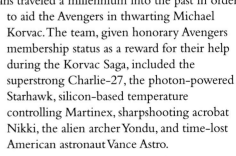

GUARDIANS OF THE GALAXY

The Guardians were a band of superpowered adventurers from the 31st century who were genetically altered to survive in the harsh atmospheres of other planets throughout our solar system. The so-called "Guardians of the Galaxy" fought to free their era from the alien Badoon. The Guardians traveled a millennium into the past in order to aid the Avengers in thwarting Michael Korvac. The team, given honorary Avengers membership status as a reward for their help during the Korvac Saga, included the superstrong Charlie-27, the photon-powered Starhawk, silicon-based temperature controlling Martinex, sharpshooting acrobat Nikki, the alien archer Yondu, and time-lost American astronaut Vance Astro.

THE AVENGERS
Vol.1 #89

"If the Nega-Power within Captain Marvel builds to a critical mass... there will be no choice for any of us!"
The Vision

Main Characters: Quicksilver; the Scarlet Witch; the Vision
Main Supporting Characters: Captain Marvel (Mar-Vell); Rick Jones
Main Locations: Miami; New York City; Avengers Mansion; the Baxter Building; the Negative Zone

Publication Date
June 1971

Editor in Chief
Stan Lee

Cover Artist
Sal Buscema

Writer
Roy Thomas

Penciler
Sal Buscema

Inker
Sam Grainger

Colorist
Uncredited

BACKGROUND

The Avengers had featured epic tales before, but Marvel's flagship title went cosmic in its eighty-ninth issue as scripter Roy Thomas began an unprecedented nine-part storyline, the galaxy-spanning Kree-Skrull War! Earth was ground zero in a cataclysmic conflict between the alien Kree and Skrull races, and the planet's only hope was the Avengers! In this pivotal issue, the prelude to a clash of empires, the team raced against time to prevent the Kree warrior known as Captain Marvel from unwittingly destroying Earth. Little did any of the participants know that many light-years away, forces conspired to spark a war of worlds that would raise the stakes of star-spanning Avengers stories forever after!

The events leading up to the great Kree-Skrull War began on Earth in Miami, Florida **(1)**. As Captain Marvel set off on his secretive mission, the Kree warrior did not realize that three Avengers—Quicksilver, the Scarlet Witch, and the Vision—were in close pursuit **(2)**!

Determined to carry out his plan, Mar-Vell would not yield to the Avengers, who attempted to warn him of a catastrophe in the making! Captain Marvel proved to be more than a match for the three powerful Avengers **(3)**, but did not anticipate being blind-sided by the one Earthling closest to him in mind and body: Rick Jones! Rick waylaid Mar-Vell just in time, **(4)** zapping the Kree hero unconscious with a ray gun **(5)**. With Mar-Vell subdued, the Avengers and Jones transported him inside their Quinjet to the nearby Cape Kennedy Hospital, where scientists were on standby with special equipment designed to siphon off dangerous Negative Radiation building to critical mass within Mar-Vell **(6)**!

But what had made Captain Marvel into a ticking time bomb threatening to destroy the entire Earth? In flashback, it was revealed that previous to his flight to Miami, Mar-Vell had switched places with Rick Jones in order to escape the Negative Zone and attempt to end his banishment with the aid of the same technology that allowed the Fantastic Four's Reed Richards to come and go within the Zone as he pleased **(7)**. Unfortunately, Mar-Vell's tampering with machinery inside the Fantastic Four's Baxter Building Headquarters allowed the dreadful being known as Annihilus to cross the interdimensional gateway between the Negative Zone and Earth **(8)**!

Captain Marvel and the Avengers were able to prevent Annihilus from rampaging across Earth, but Mar-Vell's own escape from the Zone became known to the Supreme Intelligence, ruler of the Kree Empire **(9)** and the scheming Ronan the Accuser **(10)**! Ronan plotted revenge on Mar-Vell by unleashing an omni-powered Kree Sentry, a robotic engine of destruction that would destroy anyone and anything that stood between it and Captain Marvel **(11)**! Meanwhile, worlds away, Ronan's attempts to seize Kree rule from the Supreme Intelligence set the stage for the universe-shaking Kree-Skrull War!

The Story

Longtime Avengers ally Rick Jones shared a unique bond with Captain Marvel, who could escape banishment to the Negative Zone by trading places with Jones for a few hours at a time. However, on this occasion, Mar-Vell had a desperate plan to leave the Negative Zone PERMANENTLY!

"He heeds but one command—has but one goal... That goal: KILL CAPTAIN MARVEL... and all who stand beside him!"

Ronan the Accuser

81

THE KREE-SKRULL WAR

BATTLE BEGINS...

When Ronan the Accuser usurped the power of the Kree's Supreme Intelligence, a chain of events was set in motion that would lead to the Kree-Skrull War. Both races regarded Earth as a world of strategic importance. After Ronan came into conflict with the Avengers, Skrulls manipulated the media to discredit the Avengers. They also managed to capture Captain Marvel, the Scarlet Witch, and Quicksilver—although the Vision escaped. Events soon escalated into a cosmic battle with the fate of both empires—and the Earth—resting on the outcome.

Ronan succeeded in turning the Avengers into cavemen.

PLAN ATAVUS

Kree warrior Ronan the Accuser came to Earth after escaping imprisonment. He sought to initiate Plan Atavus, which would transform humanity into cavemen so the Earth could be used by the Kree as a staging post for their assault on the Skrull Empire.

◀ SENATOR H. WARREN CRADDOCK

When details of the Avengers' fight against Ronan was printed in the newspapers, Senator H. Warren Craddock urged the Avengers to disband. The Senator and three Avengers were eventually revealed to be a Skrull infiltrators who disbanded the team.

"You have disgraced the name of the Avengers. Go then and be Avengers no more!"
Thor

ANT-MAN SAVES VISION

When the Vision escaped from the Skrulls, he collapsed on entering Avengers Mansion. Hank Pym, once again in the identity of Ant-Man, shrunk to microscopic size to enter the Vision's body in an attempt to repair his friend. Ant-Man was successful and the Vision was able to tell his teammates that Quicksilver, the Scarlet Witch, and Captain Marvel had been captured.

THE OMNI WAVE PROJECTOR

When Captain Marvel and Carol Danvers escaped from Skrull captivity, Mer-Vell built an Omni Wave Projector to warn his fellow Kree of the Skrull attack. The device allowed Kree to confer across their interstellar empire—but in alien hands it could also be used as a deadly weapon. When Mar-Vell realized that Carol Danvers was the Super Skrull, he destroyed the Projector to prevent the Skrulls gaining the technology.

MANDROIDS!

Senator Craddock used deadly Mandroids to attack the Avengers. He didn't realize they had been designed by Tony Stark, who managed to shut them down.

MAD MAX

The war also engulfed the Inhumans as Maximus the Mad teamed up with the Kree after they helped overthrow his brother Black Bolt. Triton turned to the Avengers for help. After helping the Inhumans stop Maximus and restore Black Bolt to the throne, they used an Inhuman spaceship to blast into space in search of their captured teammates.

The Supreme Intelligence was an organic computer made up from the Kree's greatest minds.

With the help of the Supreme Intelligence, Rick Jones was able to access amazing mental powers. He unleashed copies of famous heroes from Earth's Golden Age and froze both enemy Kree and Skrull, bringing the war to an end...

Jones also transformed Craddock into his Skrull form. The alien was beaten to death by an angry mob.

1970s ADVENTURES

THE BRIDE OF ULTRON

JOCASTA

Captain America, Beast, the Scarlet Witch, and Wonder Man were felled by Ultron's coma-inducing encephalo-beam! Things looked grim but Wonder Man recovered quickly, leading the remaining active Avengers (including Thor, Iron Man, and Black Panther) to join him in a desperate search for Ant-Man and the Wasp, both abducted by Ultron. Ultron built a mechanical mate using Janet Pym's psyche to bring to life robot Jocasta!

Ultron erased parts of Hank Pym's memory, manipulating Pym's alter-ego Ant-Man into battling his teammates! Ultimately, Ultron needed Pym to transfer the Wasp's consciousness into Jocasta.

THE WASP

After tracking Ultron to a facility in Long Island owned by Tony Stark, the remaining Avengers fought to liberate their teammates and force Ultron to reverse the effects of the encephalo-beam that left Cap, the Scarlet Witch, and Beast in coma-like states!

Ultimately, Iron Man threatened to destroy the inert Jocasta with his repulsor rays. Unwilling to call the armored Avenger's bluff, Ultron fled, leaving behind a still-crazed Ant-Man. Janet was saved, and Jocasta—who was built to join Ultron's war on humanity—found a purpose with the Avengers as a provisional member!

THE NEFARIA TRILOGY

Still reeling from their battle with Ultron, the Avengers barely had a moment to rest. Count Luchino Nefaria, a member of the Maggia crime syndicate, had previously used high-tech devices on his superpowered Ani-Men to bedevil Earth's Mightiest Heroes. This time, however, Count Nefaria hatched a scheme to give himself near omnipotent powers stolen from the Lethal Legion. Now more powerful than the combined might of the Avengers, Nefaria wasn't satisfied with being superpowered. He wanted to live forever!

Thor hurled his mighty hammer at Nefaria. But the Count was happy—he wanted to learn the secrets of Thor's immortality!

Unknown to the villains of the Lethal Legion, Nefaria enabled Erik Josten (Power Man) to spring fellow Legionnaires the Living Laser and Whirlwind from prison.

Yellowjacket unleashed the Vision from a restorative tank to join the fray. The Vision turned his body diamond-hard and struck Nefaria!

The daughter of mercenary Gustav Brandt, Mantis was raised by Kree aliens masquerading on Earth as monks. Brandt, who was blinded in a fire that killed Mantis' mother.

THE CELESTIAL MADONNA

Time-traveling Kang wanted to find the being prophesized to mother a Celestial Messiah who would bring peace to the universe. As it turned out, Avengers associate Mantis was the Celestial Madonna, and she was saved from Kang's wrath by the Swordsman, who sacrificed himself so that his lover would live to fulfill the prophecy. Fortunately, the Cotati aliens reanimated the Swordsman and he fulfilled his own predestined role in the story by fathering the Celestial Messiah.

Kang's own future-self Immortus presided over the strangest nuptials in Marvel history as the android Vision married the mutant Scarlet Witch, and Celestial Madonna Mantis wed the green-glowing resurrected Swordsman.

THE AVENGERS-DEFENDERS WAR

When Loki and the dread Dormammu tricked the Avengers and Defenders into searching for the six missing pieces of the Evil Eye, a powerful object that would allow them to conquer the Earth, the two teams soon came into conflict with each other. Various battles erupted between members as Thor battled Hulk, Captain America faced Prince Namor, and the Silver Surfer fought the Vision and the Scarlet Witch. When the heroes learned of the deception, they joined forces in a desperate attempt to stop the villains' plans.

As the Avengers and Defenders searched for the Evil Eye, Thor fought the Incredible Hulk, little realizing his half brother Loki was behind his quest.

ULTRON

"YOU MAY HAVE ELUDED ME THIS TIME, AVENGERS... BUT THERE ARE OTHER WAYS OF STRIKING AT YOU... YOU SHALL ALL DIE... BY THE HAND OF ULTRON-5!"

He was supposed to be "a faltering step on the path to synthetic life," but Hank Pym's robot had a will of its own. Ultron also had an implacable hatred of the human race and the Avengers in particular.

While the Siege of Asgard raged, Ultron, calling himself Ultron Pym, tried to use the Avengers' Infinite Mansion to conquer the universe. Hank Pym stopped Ultron by cyber-marrying him to Jocasta.

Ultron-15 wiped out the people of Slorenia with robotic forces, including an army of past Ultrons. The Avengers led the fight back.

Ultron used Iron Man's armor to create a female version who looked like the Wasp.

A possible future might have belonged to Ultron if a host of heroes and villains had not banded together against him. But another future could still be his to rule...

The Genocidal Robot

Ultron was a Frankenstein monster that turned on his own creator, Hank Pym. The scientist had been attempting to perfect a workable robot when it suddenly called him Father and attacked him, shouting: "The day you created me, you sealed your own irreversible doom!" Rapidly upgrading himself, Ultron wiped Pym's memories and left, leaving Pym's lab in ruins. Ultron returned, repaired the lab, and upgraded himself to Ultron-5. Posing as the Crimson Cowl, Ultron-5 collected a gang, the Masters of Evil, to attack the Avengers, and even hypnotized Jarvis to pose as the Crimson Cowl. Ultron-5 was smashed by a creation of his own, the Vision, but, significantly, Ultron's head survived intact.

Ultron re-emerged as Ultron-6 with an adamantium body; he was recreated as Ultron-7 by the villain Maximus; as Ultron-8, he made himself a robot bride, Jocasta, who, to Ultron's chagrin, proved loyal to the Avengers. Time after time the Avengers defeated Ultron, but the would-be, world-conquering robot always returned, upgraded, to threaten humanity anew. Ultron's longing for more power led him to interface with Iron Man's armor and briefly turn himself into a female version that resembled a metal-skinned version of his "mother," the Wasp.

Pym eventually enabled the love-hungry robot to wed Jocasta on condition that Ultron exile himself to outer space. But Ultron will return. And when he does, it will be apocalyptic!

Ultron first appeared in Avengers #54 (July 1968) posing as The Crimson Cowl.

Pym's robot turned violent and called him "Daddy." The awful guilt of creating Ultron would haunt Pym down the years.

The Vision, Ultron-5's "son," made himself incorporeal to shatter Ultron.

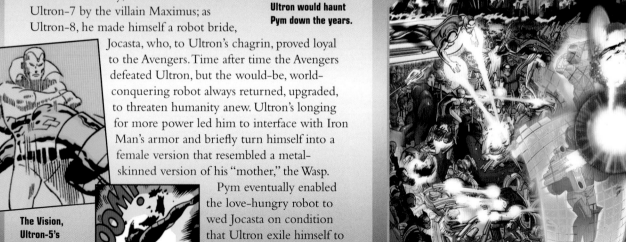

KEY DATA

REAL NAME Ultron

OCCUPATION Would-be world or universe conqueror

AFFILIATIONS The Masters of Evil, Phalanx, the Lethal Legion, Sons of Yinsen

POWERS/WEAPONS Hank Pym's intelligence, but without conscience; keeps upgrading and improving on original design; near-indestructible adamantium armor; utilizing Pym technology, can communicate remotely with other machines (computers, war platforms, robots); can hypnotize humans or place them in a deep coma with an encephalo beam; ionic shock blast for close combat; energy projection; flight.

Hypnotizing encephalo-beam.

Concussion blasters in palms.

JOCASTA AND ALKHEMA
Ultron-8's desire for a mate led him to create Jocasta in the image of his creator Hank Pym's wife, the Wasp. Jocasta turned against Ultron and became the Avengers' ally. Ultron-14 created another "bride," Alkhema, using Mockingbird's brain patterns. Disagreeing with Ultron over how best to wipe out humanity, she, too, betrayed him in the end.

"A WORLD OF MECHANICAL LIFE—A WORLD OF MY OFFSPRING, MY CHILDREN... ALL LINKED TO ME...!"

Ultron envisioned a world peopled by a new robot race, linked by the communication technology of his "father," Hank Pym. To prevent himself from becoming bored, he aimed to base his robots on the brain patterns of the Avengers he felt were his "family": Hank Pym, the Wasp, the Vision, Wonder Man, the Scarlet Witch (the Vision's closest kin), and Ultron's first human "connection," the Grim Reaper.

THE KORVAC SAGA

Korvac was from Earth's future where the alien Badoon turned him into a cyborg. Fleeing to the present, he gained god-like powers that endangered reality!

Korvac reshaped himself into the form of a perfect human after gaining cosmic powers from Galactus' base-ship.

FROM THE FUTURE...

Michael Korvac was born in the 31st century, the same era as the Guardians of the Galaxy. After Earth was invaded by the alien Badoon, Korvac became a collaborator and was turned into a cyborg. He escaped to the present day after being used as a pawn in the plans of the Grandmaster, an Elder of the Universe. Korvac located the base-ship of Galactus and assimilated knowledge and technology so advanced that it gave him god-like powers. He remade himself as a perfect human being and moved to Earth with a plan to reshape the planet into the perfect world. The Guardians of the Galaxy followed Korvac back to the present and turned to the Avengers for help. Starhawk was the first hero to locate Korvac, but before he could warn his fellow heroes, he was disintegrated and instantly reconstructed—no longer able to perceive Korvac. The Collector (another Elder of the Universe) empowered his daughter, Carina, to stop Korvac.

An Elder of the Universe, the Collector tried to save the Avengers from Korvac by adding them to his alien zoo. The Avengers managed to escape and Korvac struck.

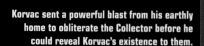

Korvac sent a powerful blast from his earthly home to obliterate the Collector before he could reveal Korvac's existence to them.

Carina fell in love with Korvac and the two were married. They lived in Forest Hills and used their powers to escape the perception of other superpowered beings. The Collector, worried about Korvac's plans, attempted to save the Avengers by adding them to his vast menagerie. The plan failed and before the Collector could warn the heroes of the danger, Korvac obliterated him.

Iron Man eventually tracked Korvac to his Forest Hills home but the heroes only realized the truth when Starhawk was unable to perceive Korvac. A huge fight ensued. Korvac, whose power seemed unstoppable, killed wave after wave of heroes, with even Captain America falling. As Iron Man and the surviving Avengers launched one last desperate attack, Korvac reached out for Carina only to see doubt and fear in her eyes. Korvac chose to end his own life——with Carina following soon after. With his last breath, Korvac used his remaining energy to bring the dead heroes back to life. The danger was over, but only Moondragon realized the truth—that Korvac had had the potential to bring peace to the whole universe.

Korvac was close to destroying the Avengers when he saw doubt in Carina's eyes. The shock made him take his own life. The Avengers were victorious and the danger was at an end.

Carina used Thor's hammer to take her own life and died next to her husband, Korvac.

"YOU WILL RECALL NOUGHT OF THE TERRIBLE DEED WE HAVE DONE! YOU AND THE OTHERS WILL BELIEVE THE AVENGERS HAVE EARNED A GREAT TRIUMPH... BUT I WILL REMEMBER FOREVER!"
Moondragon

While Korvac brought the dead heroes back to life, many were seriously injured and required emergency treatment from Thor's alter-ego, Dr. Donald Blake.

the 1980s

The 1980s saw the entire world order change with the fall of the Eastern Bloc. In light of the changing times, the Avengers' role seemed greater than ever as they faced threats not just from Earth but beyond time and space!

The 1980s brought more heroes to the ranks of the Avengers than ever before. Powerful deities like Thor and Hercules joined rookie heroes such as Quasar and Monica Rambeau, the new Captain Marvel. Over the course of the decade, Marvel released two new continuing Avengers books: *West Coast Avengers* and *Solo Avengers* (later titled *Avengers Spotlight*). The start of the decade also saw a dark time for Hank Pym as he attacked his wife, the Wasp, and was court-martialed by his teammates after injuring a foe who had stopped fighting. Creatively, the decade also saw Marvel's writers triumph again. David Michelinie, Steve Englehart, and Roger Stern all enjoyed successful runs on the title, joined by artists such as Al Milgrom, John Buscema, Tom Palmer, and Paul Ryan. John Byrne returned to *The Avengers* as a writer and artist and, by the decade's end, was guiding the adventures of both the East and West Coast teams. In the *West Coast Avengers*, Byrne also revealed the terrible secret of the Scarlet Witch's children, setting the scene for the insanity that claimed her twenty years later...

OVERLEAF

When Kang saved the life of his dead wife, Ravonna, he learned that various alternate Kangs existed. The Kangs went to war, killing alternate versions until only one "Prime Kang" remained. It was a conflict the Avengers were soon caught up in.

ROGER STERN-WRITER / JOHN BUSCEMA-BREAKDOWNS
TOM PALMER-FINISHED ART / JIM NOVAK-LETTERER
CHRISTIE SCHEELE-COLORIST/MARK GRUENWALD-EDITOR
JIM SHOOTER-EDITOR-IN-CHIEF

1980S NEW MEMBERS

By the 1980s, the Avengers were the world's most trusted team of Super Heroes. A number of new heroes joined during the decade. Many proved to be important members of the team, but some proved to be mentally unstable. Others, such as Dr. Druid, fell under the power and control of their enemies.

MOCKINGBIRD

Bobbi Morse was a SHIELD agent before taking on the identity of Mockingbird. She joined the Avengers after meeting Hawkeye and helped to form the West Coast team. After spending time as a prisoner of the Skrulls, she was freed and rejoined the Avengers.

STARFOX

Eros is the youngest son of Mentor, an Eternal living on Titan. He first met the Avengers when he helped the team defeat his brother, Thanos. When he later joined the Avengers, the Wasp suggested he change he name to the more heroic Starfox.

CAPTAIN MARVEL

Monica Rambeau worked for the New Orleans Harbor Patrol when she was hit be extra-dimensional energy from a terrorist's weapons. The press called her Captain Marvel. She was a popular member of the Avengers, becoming team leader.

FIREBIRD

When a meteor nearly hit Bonita Juarez, she gained control over unearthly energy. Firebird first helped the Avengers fight Master Pandemonium and has fought with the team a number of times since. She is also a member of the Rangers, a Texas-based team.

USAGENT

John Walker was selected by the U.S. government to replace Steve Rogers as Captain America. After quitting the role, he became USAgent and joined the West Coast Avengers. He later became head of security for the Raft.

TIGRA

Greer Nelson was once the costumed hero known as the Cat. A race of cat-people transformed Greer into a more feline form. She fought in both East and West Coast Avengers before teaching at the Avengers Academy.

JOCASTA

Ultron crerated Jocasta to be his bride, programming her with the personality of Janet Van Dyne (the Wasp). She turned on her creator to fight alongside the Avengers. She has been destroyed several times, but always manages to return.

WAR MACHINE

Jim Rhodes was a member of the U.S. Airforce and became a close confidant of Tony Stark. He took on the role of Iron Man when Stark's alcoholism made him unable to wear the armor. Over the years, Jim has upgraded his original armor to suit his military nature. Jim was a charter member of the West Coast Avengers and has recently fought as part of the Secret Avengers.

SHE-HULK

When Jennifer Walters was shot, she was saved by a blood transfusion from her cousin, Bruce Banner. The blood transformed her into She-Hulk. Jen remains intelligent when she becomes She-Hulk. She has been a member of the Avengers and the Fantastic Four.

HUMAN TORCH

The original Human Torch was an android created by Phineas T. Horton in the 1930s. It later adopted the name Jim Hammond and was believed to have burnt itself out. The Scarlet Witch revived the android, who went on to join the West Coast Avengers.

DR. DRUID

Anthony Druid was trained by the Ancient One. He joined the Avengers after helping them to defeat the Masters of Evil. He became a pawn of Terminatrix, who used him to attack the team. He was killed by Damian Hellstrom, Son of Satan.

QUASAR

Wendell Vaughn was a SHIELD agent who used the mysterious Quantum Bands against agents of AIM, becoming Quasar. He manned the Avengers deep space satellite and went on to lead the Annihilators.

SUB-MARINER

Prince Namor is the child of a human father and Atlantean mother. He fought alongside Captain America as part of the Invaders during World War II and more recently as a member of the Avengers. He has also been in the Defenders and the X-Men after accepting his mutant heritage.

MR. FANTASTIC

Reed Richards is a scientific genius and leader of the Fantastic Four. Reed and his wife, Sue Richards, briefly joined the Avengers while taking a leave of absence from the Fantastic Four. Reed has worked with Tony Stark on a number of plans to make the world a better place— and safer from Super Villians.

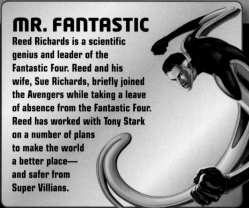

INVISIBLE WOMAN

Sue Storm gained her powers after joining her future husband Reed Richards, her brother Johnny, and friend Ben Grimm on an experimental spaceflight. The four were bombarded by cosmic rays, which gave Sue powers of invisibility— including invisible forcefields.

MOON KNIGHT

Marc Spector became Moon Knight after his life was saved by followers of the Egyptian God Khonshu. While he prefers to work alone, he has been a member of the West Coast Avengers and Steve Rogers' covert Secret Avengers team.

MARRINA

Marrina is an alien who hatched from an egg after being found by fisherman Thomas Isherwood. She became a member of Alpha Flight and fought alongside the Avengers after marrying Prince Namor, the Sub-Mariner. She recently returned to Alpha Flight.

D-MAN

Dennis Dunphy was a professional wrestler who had gained special powers from the Power Broker. He based his outfit on Daredevil and Wolverine. After several adventures with the Avengers, he joined the American military.

THE THING

The Fantastic Four's resident powerhouse nearly became a member of the West Coast Avengers during a leave of absence from the Fantastic Four. Years later, Luke Cage asked him to join his team. Ben Grimm (the Thing) then started to split his time between the Avengers and the Fantastic Four.

YELLOWJACKET

Rita DeMara became the second Yellowjacket after stealing a copy of the costume from Avengers Mansion. She was a member of the Masters of Evil, but later reformed and fought alongside the Avengers. She joined the Guardians of the Galaxy but was later killed by Kang.

GILGAMESH

A member of the Eternals, Gilgamesh has been known by several names over the centuries including the Forgotten One. When demons invaded Earth, he fought alongside Captain America and remained a member of the Avengers. After dying while with the Avengers he was later reborn in Brazil.

THE WASP

THE SCARLET WITCH

HAWKEYE

Hawkeye was full of enthusiasm when he formed the team with his wife Mockingbird, but the adventure ended tragically.

WEST COAST AVENGERS

Master Pandemonium's search for his soul brought heartbreak to the Scarlet Witch. Her twin sons were two of its missing pieces!

WONDER MAN

TIGRA

"Who will answer Hawkeye's call to join the new team?"

ORIGINS

Captain America had wanted the Avengers' membership to be limited to just six. But over the years, membership grew. New chairman the Vision decided to utilize this growth by setting up a California expansion team—the West Coast Avengers. Newlyweds Hawkeye and Mockingbird were authorized to form the team. Its base was a high-tech compound with a satellite link to Avengers Mansion. The Vision appointed Hawkeye leader, and arranged for Tigra, Wonder Man, and Iron Man (secretly Jim Rhodes) to join. However, the lineup was rarely stable, and would include neurotic scientist Hank Pym, the Wasp, the Thing, USAgent, the Scarlet Witch, and the Vision. The latter two joined following a split between Hawkeye and Mockingbird over whether the Avengers were entitled to use lethal force—Mockingbird had been attacked by Phantom Rider and let him die.

The team fought foes old and new—new ones included the demonic Master Pandemonium and the sentient super-computer Dominus. However, much of the West Coast Avengers' focus was inward, concerning Hawkeye and Mockingbird's stormy relationship and the Scarlet Witch and the Vision's individual issues and marital problems. Hawkeye resigned, grief-stricken, after Mockingbird died battling Mephisto and the Lethal Legion. The WCA subsequently broke up.

Previously believed deceased, the Human Torch joined the WCA and met up with the Vision, who had been created from his android body. By this time, the Vision had been rebuilt without emotions. He was thus unable to give his wife, the Scarlet Witch, the support she badly needed.

GREAT LAKES AVENGERS

Hawkeye and Mockingbird reluctantly agreed to back a new band of mutant heroes, the Great Lakes Avengers. The GLA went on to aid the WCA, as well as having their own adventures. The GLA was led by the aptly named Mr. Immortal, and included supermodel Ashley Crawford (Big Bertha) could control her body mass, Dinah Soar (who loved Mr. Immortal), a flying alien with a hypersonic cry, Flatman, with his two-dimensional elastic body, and Doorman, who could utilize the Darkforce so objects passed though him and what he stood near—ideal for making an unforced entry.

THE FALL OF HANK PYM

An Avengers founding member, Hank Pym was a brilliant scientist. His brave, loving, and beautiful wife, Jan always stood by his side—the Wasp to his Yellowjacket. But something was eating Hank, an insecurity born from the pressure of being a Super Hero. So began a downward spiral that would lead to crackup, divorce, criminality, and jail.

COURT MARTIAL

Hank's reckless actions had endangered the lives of the team. He had to hand in his Avengers priority ID pending a court martial.

While Iron Man recalled Hank's troubled past, in particular his invention of the robot Ultron, Hank sought refuge in his lab. He was determined to redeem himself in his teammates' eyes. Ultron may have been a disaster, but this time would be different. He, Hank Pym, would be triumphant...

Hank worked night and day to build another robot, Sal. He planned to unleash Sal during the court martial then step in and save the day. Hank would be hailed a hero.

During the hearing, Sal turned on Hank himself and Jan saved his life. Utterly humiliated, Hank left Avengers Mansion.

*"GUESS I'LL GO NOW...
GUESS I'LL GO."*

—HANK PYM

VIOLENT OUTBURST

Worried that Hank was overworking, Jan went to check on him. The robot Sal grabbed her, forcing Hank to disable it. Hank then revealed his crazy plan to deceive the Avengers into reinstating him. Jan's protests drove him into a violent fury.

HARSH WORDS AND ACTIONS

Tension had already surfaced in private. Hank spurned Jan in public: "I don't need your butlers, your cars or your money—and I don't need you!" During a mission to intercept the Elf Queen, Hank, desperate to be the star, used unnecessary violence, breaking the Avengers' Code. Hank might have been killed had Jan not saved him—which only made him resent her more!

*"DON'T YOU SEE?...IT'S MY ONLY CHANCE
TO REDEEM MYSELF! IT'S THE ONLY WAY!"*

—HANK PYM

ROBBER AND JAILBIRD

Hank agreed to fit an artificial arm to Egghead's injured, estranged niece Trisha Starr for $500,000. Egghead had once tried to use the powers of Trisha's mind to conquer the world, causing her great suffering. He now claimed he wanted to make amends. The arm gave Egghead complete control over Trisha. Furthermore, Egghead threatened to kill Trisha if Hank refused to help steal the government's stockpile of Adamantium. The heist was thwarted by the Avengers and Hank ended up in jail, pending trial.

While in jail, Hank heard that Tony Stark was having a much-publicized love affair with Jan.

A free man once more, Hank spoke up on behalf of his old comrade Hawkeye. The Avengers asked Hank to become an associate member, but he refused, aware that he was not cut out to be a Super Hero. After a poignant parting with Jan, Hank bid goodbye to the Avengers.

"I GUESS I BETTER BE GOING NOW."

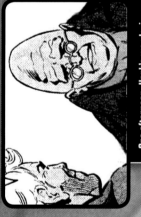

One afternoon, Hank's wanderings took him to a downtown bar. Little did he know that he'd been followed by Egghead, a wanted criminal and one of his oldest foes. The scientific mastermind made Hank a tempting offer he couldn't afford to refuse.

OUTCAST

Divorced from Jan, no longer an Avenger, endlessly replaying recent events in his mind, Hank was truly down on his luck. His worried former teammates hoped he would get in touch. In fact, Hank tried to phone Tony Stark, but was too broke to make the call.

FINAL REDEMPTION

Hank's trial was interrupted by Egghead's new gang, the Masters of Evil, who staged a "rescue" to further incriminate Hank. Egghead wanted to exploit Hank's scientific expertise in his latest dastardly scheme and believed that Hank had no choice but to obey. While the Avengers assembled outside Egghead's house, Hank used his knowledge to turn the tables on the Masters of Evil. Hank then got to grips with Egghead, watched approvingly by Hawkeye.

Hank believed he had knocked out Egghead, but Egghead pulled a gun and would have killed Hank, if it wasn't for Hawkeye. The Avenger's arrow accidentally brought about Egghead's death, breaking the Avengers' Code.

UNDER SIEGE

The son of the original Baron Zemo took on his father's mantle and formed a new Masters of Evil—one containing some of the most powerful villains the Avengers had ever faced. He came close to defeating the Avengers and left Hercules and Jarvis close to death...

ZEMO SCHEMES

Baron Zemo's new Masters of Evil included some of the deadliest bad guys the Avengers had ever faced. The new team included Yellowjacket, Mr. Hyde, Blackout, the Wrecking Crew, Giant-Man, and the Fixer. Absorbing Man and Titania helped free Moonstone from police custody.

INVASION

When Jarvis was left alone in Avengers Mansion, the Masters of Evil invaded, capturing Jarvis and taking control of the mansion. As individual Avengers returned home, the villains were waiting. Captain Marvel was neutralized by Blackout while Captain America and the Black Knight were captured. A drugged Hercules was beaten into unconsciousness. Blackout (controlled by Zemo) used his Darkforce power to seal off the mansion from the outside world. Convinced Hercules was dead, the villains threw his body out of the mansion.

The Olympian was alive but in a critical condition. Absorbing Man and Titania were dispatched to finish the job but the Wasp and Ant-Man stopped them. It was time for the Avengers to strike back…

ZEMO AND THE MASTERS OF EVIL

"TOGETHER WE CAN UTTERLY DEFEAT WHOEVER RISES TO OPPOSE US! WE OUT-NUMBER THE AVENGERS. FOR ALL THEIR POWER THEY WILL FALL BEFORE OUR SUPERIOR NUMBERS."

BARON ZEMO

After Jarvis was captured, he was brutally tortured by the Masters of Evil. Mr. Hyde gained special pleasure in torturing the defenseless man—knowing that Jarvis' screams of agony was mental torture to the captured Captain America and Black Knight. The punishment nearly killed Jarvis and left him traumatized, long after the siege had ended.

FINAL BATTLE

As the Wasp launched a counter strike, Black Knight was able to recover his Ebony Blade and free Captain America. Together the two heroes made short work of Mr. Hyde. Captain Marvel escaped from Blackout thanks to the Shroud sharing the same Darkforce power with the villain and was able to accompany the Wasp, Thor, Ant-Man, and Dr. Druid as they invaded the mansion. The Avengers faced the Masters of Evil in a ferocious final battle that left the mansion in ruins…

> "I've known torture, Zemo. I've endured the worst the Third Reich had to offer. If there's one thing life has taught me, it's never to give up!"
>
> **CAPTAIN AMERICA**

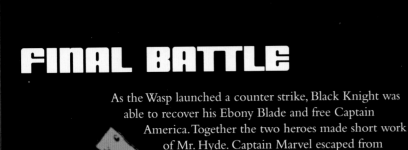

ZEMO DIES

At the end of the siege, Captain America confronted Baron Zemo on the mansion's hangar deck. As the two men fought, Zemo blamed Captain America for his father's death. Captain America realized Zemo was mad and tried to reason with him. As Cap defended himself from attack, Zemo stumbled back, falling from the hangar to the ground. It looked like Zemo was dead, but the villain would return to plague the Avengers again and later formed the Thunderbolts with many of the villains who had been part of his Masters of Evil.

The only photo of Cap's mother was destroyed by the Masters of Evil during their attack.

BLACKOUT

One of the most powerful members of the new Masters of Evil was Blackout. Moonstone and Zemo manipulated the villain into working with them. When Dr. Druid freed him from their control, Blackout fought back against Zemo, dying in the process from a massive cerebral hemorrhage.

"WE HAVE TO HELP EACH OTHER SALVAGE WHAT WE CAN FROM THE PAST, AND REBUILD FOR THE FUTURE."

"YOU'RE RIGHT MONICA. C'MON, LET'S GET OUT OF HERE."

THE AVENGERS
Vol.1 #280

MARVEL
THE AVENGERS

75¢ US
280
JUNE
02458

"TO SERVE NO MORE..."

"The fear will always be with me... but I expect that fear is always with the Avengers as well. It's part of being an Avenger." Jarvis

Main Characters: Jarvis; Iron Man; Hulk; Thor; Ant-Man; the Wasp; Captain America,
Main Supporting Characters: Unnamed Physician
Main Locations: New York City; Avengers Mansion

Publication Date
June 1987

Editor in Chief
Jim Shooter

Cover Artists
Bob Hall, Tom Palmer

Writer
Bob Harras

Penciler
Bob Hall

Inker
Kyle Baker

Colorist
Max Scheele

BACKGROUND

In an action-packed comic book like *The Avengers*, an occasional "change-of-pace" story, like issue #280, can remind readers that Earth's Mightiest Heroes are really just flesh and blood beneath their colorful costumes.

"Faithful Servant" is a tale told from the perspective of the Avengers' faithful butler Edwin Jarvis. Jarvis might just be ready to give up serving the team following a near fatal beating at the hands of the monstrous Mr. Hyde a few issues back in *The Avengers #275*. With severe head, eye, and leg injuries—not to mention potential brain damage—Jarvis faced the reality that he may never walk again, let alone oversee the day-to-day running of Avengers Mansion. As he convalesced in his hospital bed, Jarvis reflected on his time with Earth's Mightiest Heroes, revealing the family he has come to care for while catering to their needs as a true gentleman's gentleman.

The Story

With the Masters of Evil on the attack yet again, the Avengers had their hands full. Baron Zemo took his personal vendetta against Captain America to the next level by ordering Mr. Hyde to savagely beat Jarvis before the helpless hero's eyes. Several issues later, Jarvis realized that Hyde may have done far worse than cripple him...

Jarvis's personal physician delivered devastating news: given the extent of his injuries, he might suffer 90 per cent vision loss in his left eye, and he would require a cane to walk after extensive physical therapy. Most alarming of all was the possibility of brain damage **(1)**. But after the torture he suffered at the hands of Mr. Hyde, the Avengers' faithful servant was lucky just to be alive **(2)**. While his doctor recommended finding a new line of work, Jarvis's longtime employer Tony Stark offered Jarvis early retirement with full salary and benefits provided for by the Maria Stark Foundation **(3)**. "Avengers Mansion," Stark said, "is no place for a normal man." Despite the prospect of retiring to a life of leisure, Jarvis felt genuine sadness that his time with Earth's Mightiest Heroes might be at an end **(4)**. As he convalesced, Jarvis reflected on his long career as the Avengers' butler, recalling first meeting the heroes at an impromptu dinner meeting organized by Iron Man to draw up the Avengers' by-laws **(5)**. He also recalled the team's roster shift that led to Cap's "Kooky Quartet," and the time when the reformed Hawkeye had tied up Jarvis in order to plead his case for membership in the team **(6)**. Still later, Jarvis remembered being brainwashed by Ultron and forced to betray the Avengers, although he was forgiven by the team **(7)**. Jarvis fondly recalled his friendship with Earth's Mightiest Heroes, particularly the Vision, with whom he shared a love of literature **(8)**. And Jarvis also felt a pang of mourning for the Swordsman, since it was his duty as butler to box up the belongings of fallen Avengers **(9)**. Through it all, Jarvis had no regrets, even as he suffered indignities at the hands of Avengers' foes—maddened teammates like the schizophrenic Yellowjacket, and even the team's government liaison, Henry Peter Gyrich **(10)**. The breaking point for the loyal butler was perhaps his threat to resign if Tony Stark did not conquer the alcoholism that threatened to destroy everything Stark had worked for, including his heroic career as Iron Man **(11)**. In the end, Jarvis knew that despite his grievous injuries and the resulting fears he had yet to conquer, his place was where it always had been: Avengers Mansion **(12)**.

> **"Things really can't go on without me, now can they?"**
> Jarvis

103

1980s ADVENTURES

HYDRO-BASE

When their mansion was destroyed by the Masters of Evil, the Avengers used Stingray's Hydro-Base as their new headquarters. It was a floating craft disguised as an island. Hydro-Base's first known use was by the evil Dr. Hydro. By the time the Avengers occupied it, the island was under the stewardship of Stingray (Dr. Walter Newell).

WORLDWIDE VISION

After fighting and defeating Annihilus, the Vision was forced to shut down his own body to recover. The process left him mentally unbalanced but with increased capacity. He attempted to use his power to bring peace to the world by taking over all computer systems. The Avengers eventually talked him out of his insane plan, freeing him from his corrupted extra memory. The Vision then removed the Control Crystal Ultron had originally planted in his brain so he wouldn't be a danger to his allies again.

KANG LIVES

Kang's travels in time had resulted in the creation of other Kangs in divergent realities. Three Kangs formed the Council of Time and started to kill the rival Kangs. The three were also plotting against each other, with one Kang hoping the Avengers would destroy his rivals. The Avengers found themselves trapped in Limbo and under attack from Dire Wraiths and a terrified Space Phantom. As the Avengers confronted the final two Kangs, Immortus was revealed to have been manipulating events from Limbo to use the Kangs to wipe their chronal variants from existence. The surviving Kang was driven insane and lost in Limbo, Immortus seemingly victorious…

Immortus confronted the surviving Kang and revealed that he had been working to wipe all versions of Kang from the Timestream.

"NO! YOU… YOU CAN'T BE IMMORTUS… THIS IS SOME KIND OF TRICK." Kang

HEAVY METAL

The Super-Adaptoid returned to plague the Avengers and this time had a whole crew of Heavy Metal robots backing him up. The Adaptoid's plan was to gain the power of the cosmic cube, power that had been transformed into a being called Kubik. The Heavy Metal group consisted of Machine Man, a Kree Sentry, and Tess-One (Total Extermination of Super Soldiers) with a freed Awesome Android soon joining them. The Adaptoid managed to gain cosmic powers from Kubik and trapped the Avengers. Captain America (then on a leave of absence) returned to save the day, defeating the Adaptoid with logic by telling the Adaptoid that it could never be truly human as it could not die. So the Adaptoid attempted to prove Cap wrong by doing just that! Kubik removed the Adaptoid's cosmic powers, the threat having come to an end.

The Super-Adaptoid had taken on the appearance and skills of the Fixer and used them to attack the Avengers' new Hydro-Base.

Tess-One, Machine Man, Kree Sentry 459, the Super-Adaptoid, and Awesome Android called themselves Heavy Metal as they attacked the Avengers.

ASSAULT ON OLYMPUS

Zeus found Hercules near death after facing the Masters of Evil and believed the Avengers were responsible. He brought the team to Olympus and sent them to Hades as punishment. It was left to Namor the Sub-Mariner and a mysterious stranger (later revealed to be Prometheus) to free them. The resulting battle pitted the Avengers against the Gods of Olympus. Prometheus helped to restore Hercules' health and Dr. Druid used magic to restore his mind. When Hercules told Zeus what had actually happened, Zeus thanked the Avengers and banned the Olympians from ever setting foot on Earth again.

Zeus apologized to his son, Hercules after nearly killing him when Hercules tried to help his fellow Avengers.

ACTS OF VENGEANCE

It was one of Loki's boldest moves— to unite all the world's villains in one coordinated attack on their enemies. The main conspirators were the Wizard, Kingpin, Mandarin, Magneto, Dr. Doom, and the Red Skull. The Avengers' Hydro-Base was destroyed by Dr. Doom's forces. But the alliance fell apart when they started to fight amongst themselves. They were eventually defeated by the Avengers and Loki fled back to Asgard.

***"TIME TO ACCELERATE THE PROCESS AND BRING ABOUT ONCE AND FOR ALL... THE FINAL OBLITERATION OF THE ACCURSED AVENGERS."* Loki**

the **1990s**

The 1990s began with another star-spanning saga in *Operation: Galactic Storm*, reached a universe-rebooting *Onslaught* mid-decade, and came full circle to restart the *Avengers* at issue #1 before the turn of the millennium not once but TWICE!

Throughout the 1990s Earth's Mightiest Heroes continued to face battles against Kang and Ultron. New threats like the Brethren and the Gatherers tested the Avengers' resolve as the team's membership rotated almost issue-by-issue. In 1992 longtime members the Vision and the Scarlet Witch ended their unorthodox union once and for all. But even more fractious for the Avengers was the 1996 *Onslaught* crossover event that began in the X-Men family of titles. To defeat Onslaught, the Avengers and the Fantastic Four hurled themselves into the void as if leaping headlong through a siege perilous and emerged changed on the other side. Both heroic teams were relaunched in the subsequent *Heroes Reborn* series of titles spearheaded by wildly popular comics creators Rob Liefeld and Jim Lee. Fan reactions to the reimagined titles were mixed, and the stories chronicled were ultimately relegated to a "pocket universe" outside of the larger Avengers continuity. By 1998, a second *Avengers* #1 in less than three years would launch with *Heroes Return* under the auspices of fan-favorite writer Kurt Busiek and artist George Pérez.

OVERLEAF

Busiek and Pérez realized that the Avengers' core membership was a "dream team" that included Captain America, Thor, Iron Man, Giant-Man, and the Wasp. The Vision, Scarlet Witch, and Hawkeye would also rejoin to help train new members in time to face some Avengers' foes of the past disguised as newly minted heroes!

1990S NEW MEMBERS

The 1990s saw an influx of new members to the Avengers. These included reformed Super Villains the Sandman and the Eternal Sersi. It was a decade in which the team faced some of its deadliest threats, including the apocalyptical power of Onslaught, the Kree-Sh'iar War, and a betrayal from one of the Avengers' own.

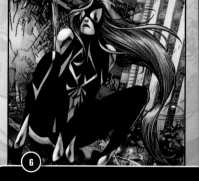

1 SERSI
The Eternal known as Sersi is believed to be several thousand years old, perhaps formerly the ancient Greek goddess Circe, a key historical figure. As an Avenger, Sersi fell in love with the Black Knight and trekked across parallel realities with him after temporary bouts of madness forced her to leave Earth for a time.

2 RAGE
Fleeing from bullies, 12-year-old Elvin Haliday jumped into a chemical-polluted creek and mutated into a superpowered adult. With increased strength, speed, and agility, Elvin became Rage and helped the Avengers fight against alien criminals, eventually joining the team. Rage was expelled when the team learned his age.

3 LIVING LIGHTNING
Miguel Santos's father was the leader of the Legion of Living Lightning. Miguel tried to follow in his footsteps, but an accident turned him into living lightning. He was tricked by Demonicus into fighting the West Coast Avengers before switching sides and joining the team.

4 CAPTAIN BRITAIN
When single mother Kelsey Leigh sacrificed her own life to protect Captain America from the Wrecking Crew, Brian Braddock made her his successor as Captain Britain. She helped the Avengers defeat Morgan Le Fay and remained with the team while coming to terms with her new life. When Brian returned as Captain Britain, she took the name Lionheart.

5 SPIDER-MAN
Bitten by an irradiated spider, Peter Parker gained superpowers, including the ability to climb walls and cling to nearly any surface, and a precognitive "spider-sense," signaling impending danger. Peter used his powers to become the heroic Spider-Man following the death of his beloved Uncle Ben, who taught him that "with great power comes great responsibility." Spider-Man divides his time between solo adventuring and membership in both the Avengers and Fantastic Four.

6 SPIDER-WOMAN
Julia Carpenter gained her powers after the Commission on Superhuman Activities experimented on her using rare Amazonian plants and spider-venom. She joined the Avengers after helping them fight the Pacific Overlords and spent time as a member of the West Coast team. She recently assumed the role of Madame Web following the original's death.

7 JACK OF HEARTS
Jack's father was a scientist who created a new energy source—Zero Fluid. When thieves killed his father, Jack was covered in the fluid. It gave him amazing and, at first, uncontrollable, energy powers. He avenged his father's death and built a containment suit. After learning his mother was an alien, Jack adventured into space. He fought alongside the Avengers against the Infinites and returned to Earth with the heroes only to later die when his powers went out of control.

8 SWORDSMAN
Philip Javert was the Swordsman on an alternative Earth. He became one of Proctor's Gatherers and attacked the Avengers before breaking free of Proctor's control and joining the team along with another ex-Gatherer, Magdalene. After helping the Squadron Supreme open a dimensional portal back to their own reality, the Swordsman left Earth with Magdalene, hoping to find a planet they could both call home.

9 STINGRAY
Oceanographer Walter Newell created an armored costume in order to capture Namor the Sub-Mariner for the U.S. government. But Newell released Namor and the two aquatic heroes became allies. As Stingray, Newell teamed up with the Avengers, letting the group move its headquarters to his Hydro-Base. He now serves the Initiative.

10 SANDMAN
William Baker (Flint Marko), was blasted with radiation at a nuclear test site, and became living sand. He used his powers as the Sandman to become a super-criminal—and a frequent foe of Spider-Man. Sandman briefly reformed and became an Avengers reserve member, but the Wizard soon turned him back to villainy.

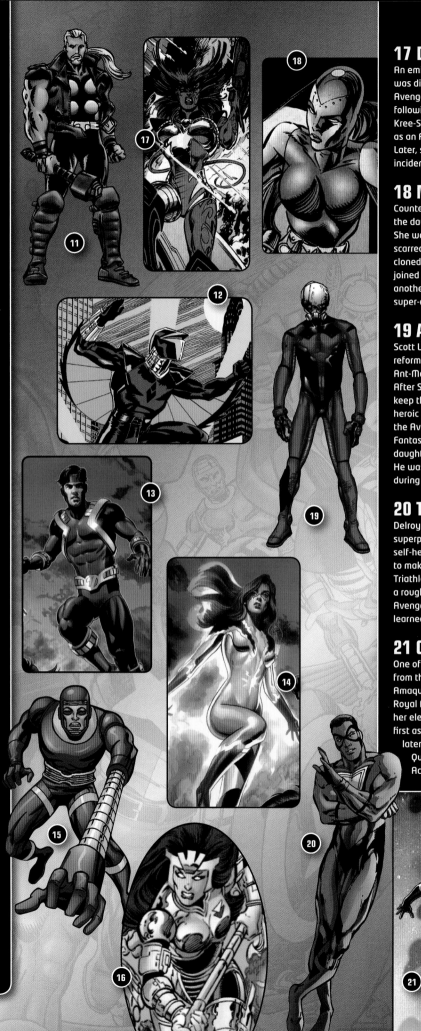

11 THUNDERSTRIKE

Architect Eric Masterson became merged with Thor after he attempted to save the Thunder God's life. He later served as an Avenger instead of Thor and wielded his own hammer, called "Thunderstrike." He sacrificed himself to save Earth and was later raised from the dead to join a fourth Legion of the Unliving.

12 DARKHAWK

When teenager Chris Powell found a mysterious amulet, it allowed him to change places with an android stored in Null Space. His consciousness was then able to operate the android. After helping the West Coast Avengers fight Klaw and Morningstar, he became a reserve member of the team. Chris recently learned that the armor was from the Fraternity of Raptors, an ancient Shi'ar peacekeeping force.

13 JUSTICE

When the teenage Vance Astrovik met his future self, Vance Astro of the Guardians of the Galaxy, his own mental powers were awakened. Vance had loved Super Heroes as a child and soon decided to use his new powers to fight crime. After years as a member of the New Warriors, the young Vance and his girlfriend Firestar were invited to join the Avengers.

14 FIRESTAR

Angelica Jones was born a mutant and developed the ability to manipulate microwaves. When her powers first appeared, a scared Angelica joined Emma Frost's Hellions. After learning of that school's sinister nature she left, eventually joining the New Warriors. She became an Avenger with her then boyfriend Vance Astrovik and helped him overcome his concerns that he wasn't good enough to fight alongside such powerful heroes.

15 MACHINE MAN

Originally called X-51, Machine Man was the last of 51 robots created by Dr. Abel Stack. Taking the human name of Aaron Stack, Machine Man fell in love with Jocasta. He first fought alongside the Avengers when the Super-Adaptoid asked him to help attack the Hydro-Base.

16 MAGDALENE

Warrior Woman Magdalene hails from the doomed Earth-9021. She once joined the Gatherers and traveled to parallel Earths with the mad Proctor to murder each world's Sersi, falsely believing the Eternal was responsible for the destruction of countless worlds. She learned the error of her ways and became an honorary member of the Avengers.

17 DEATHCRY

An emissary of the Shi'ar Empire, Deathcry was dispatched to Earth to protect the Avengers from vengeful Kree agents following the team's involvement in the Kree-Shi'ar War. The avian warrior served as an Avenger during her time on Earth. Later, she was killed in a "friendly fire" incident with Captain Universe.

18 MASQUE

Countess Giulietta Nefaria (Whitney Frost) is the daughter of Avenger's foe Count Nefaria. She wore a gilded mask to conceal her scarred face. As Madame Masque, she has cloned herself repeatedly. One of her clones joined the Avengers as "Masque," while another sided with the Hood's cadre of super-criminals.

19 ANT-MAN

Scott Lang was an electronics expert and reformed thief who stole Hank Pym's Ant-Man suit to save his daughter's life. After Scott turned himself in, Hank let him keep the costume as long as he used it for heroic purposes. Ant-Man fought alongside the Avengers and became a member of the Fantastic Four. After losing custody of his daughter, he returned to the Avengers. He was killed when Jack of Hearts exploded during the Scarlet Witch's attack on the team.

20 TRIATHLON

Delroy Garrett was a failed athlete given superpowers by the Triune, a sinister self-help group who used their connections to make Delroy (by then a hero called Triathlon) a member of the Avengers. After a rough start, Triathlon became a trusted Avenger and turned on the Triune when he learned of the group's evil intentions.

21 CRYSTAL

One of the genetically altered Inhumans from the Blue Area of the Moon, Crystalia Amaquelin Maximoff is a member of the Royal Family of Attilan. As Crystal, she used her elemental powers in defense of Earth, first as a member of the Fantastic Four and later an Avenger. She was once married to Quicksilver, but is now wed to Ronan the Accuser in an Inhuman/Kree alliance.

GALACTIC STORM

When Captain America rescued Rick Jones from the Shi'ar, he learned that the alien empire was at war with the Kree. It was a war that threatened to destroy Earth itself. The Avengers split into three teams to deal with the threat and try and to bring peace to the warring empires.

THE TEAMS

The Kree's elite strikeforce was called Starforce and included Ronan the Accuser, Ultimus, Shatterax, Supremor, and Korath the Pursuer. They served the will of the Kree leadership and took the war into the heart of the Shi'ar Imperium.

The greatest warriors of the Shi'ar Imperium became members of the Imperial Guard. Their number included Titan, Hussar, Hardball, Smasher, Astra, and Earthquake. When Starforce attacked, they protected their ruler Lilandra.

KREE MISSION
Along with Captain America, was Hawkeye (as Goliath), Iron Man, Crystal, Hercules, Black Knight, and Sersi.

The Avengers sent into the heart of the Kree Empire faced the Kree warriors known as Starforce. The team was captured and treated as prisoners of war by the Kree before they made their escape. They could only watch with horror as the Supreme Intelligence once again took control of the Kree Empire.

HOME FORCE
She-Hulk, Falcon, Mockingbird, Spider-Woman, Hank Pym, the Wasp, Gilgamesh, and USAgent.

One group of Avengers remained to protect Earth. When some Kree prisoners escaped, Dr. Minerva was revealed to be the Shi'ar Imperial Guard member Shifter. He had taken Captain Atlas' Nega-bands, and the Shi'ar's ultimate weapon was closer to completion.

SHI'AR MISSION
Thor, Wonderman, the Vision, the Scarlet Witch, Captain Marvel, Starfox, and the Living Lightning.

The Avengers sent to the Shi'ar uncovered Skrull imposters at the heart of the Empire. The Skrulls escaped—with the powerful Nega-Bomb now under their control. Their escape would lead one of the greatest mass slaughters the Universe had ever known, with billions of Kree dying.

Deathbird fought for her sister, Majestrix Lilandra, during the war, killing the Kree leadership.

Skrull infiltrators stole the Nega-Bomb and took it into the heart of the Kree Empire. The Avengers followed, but were unable to prevent the bomb from exploding.

The Supreme Intelligence believed the Nega-Bomb would help Kree evolution.

ALIEN DIPLOMACY

The two Avengers teams sent into space were soon caught up in interstellar politics and conspiracies. At the heart of the Kree Empire, Captain America's team was unable to stop Deathbird killing the Kree rulers. As she fled, the Avengers found themselves captives of the new Kree ruler—the reborn Supreme Intelligence. The Shi'ar team uncovered a Skrull conspiracy at the heart of the Imperium where a Skrull had taken on the form of Lilandra's trusted advisor and convinced her to deploy the Nega-Bomb into the heart of the Kree Empire. This vast weapon was developed from the Nega-band technology once used by Rick Jones and the original Captain Marvel. Skrull warriors made sure it was deployed and, despite the arrival of the Avengers, the bomb still exploded, killing billions and decimating the Kree. The Avengers survived the blast and learned that the war had been planned by the Supreme Intelligence. The Kree leader believed his people had reached an evolutionary dead end and wanted to restart its evolution by wiping out vast numbers. The Avengers were appalled when they realized the truth and some, including Iron Man, wanted to execute the Kree leader for war crimes. Captain America opposed this and won a team vote, only for the dissenting Avengers to try and execute the Kree leader anyway. The Supreme Intelligence escaped. The Shi'ar annexed the Kree Empire and Deathbird was given charge of the new territory. The war was at an end—but at the cost of billions of lives.

The Black Knight tried to execute the Supreme Intelligence. He was backed in his actions by several fellow Avengers, including Iron Man.

AFTERMATH

The Avengers had prevented the threat to Earth but failed to stop the near total destruction of the Kree. The Shi'ar Imperium was now the dominant force in the Universe and the Kree Empire was in ruins. The Avengers were divided—Iron Man and Captain America's views were polar opposites. While it wasn't the first time the two heroes had disagreed, it signified a change in their friendship that would reach its nadir during the civil war that occurred years later.

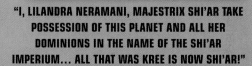

"I, LILANDRA NERAMANI, MAJESTRIX SHI'AR TAKE POSSESSION OF THIS PLANET AND ALL HER DOMINIONS IN THE NAME OF THE SHI'AR IMPERIUM… ALL THAT WAS KREE IS NOW SHI'AR!"

PROCTOR and the GATHERERS

Proctor was the Black Knight from the parallel universe of Earth-374. He traveled across the Multiverse killing alternate versions of Sersi, the Eternal who he had once loved. Working with alternate versions of Avengers called the Gatherers, he arrived on Earth-616 planning to destroy Sersi and her world once again!

Proctor bent Ute the Watcher to his will.

KILLING REALITY

Proctor originated on Earth-374 where he fell in love with fellow Avenger, the Eternal Sersi. She mind-melded with Proctor, making him her Gann Josin (the name given to an Eternal's life-mate). This connection gave Proctor a powerful psychic bond with Sersi. When Sersi grew bored of her lover and left him, Proctor used his psychic link to drive her insane. She went on to destroy their reality before Proctor killed her with his ebony blade. The power from his role as Gann Josin and the curse of his ebony blade gave Proctor immense powers. He captured an injured Watcher called Ute and became aware of the Multiverse. He then used Ute's power to traverse the Multiverse, driving each world's Sersi insane so she would destroy that reality as he killed her. By the time Proctor arrived on Earth-616 he was accompanied by the Gatherers, a powerful group of rescued heroes.

FIRST MEETING

Proctor first met Sersi when she decided to join the Avengers of his reality. On their Earth, the Avengers were based in New Amsterdam and Proctor was their leader. Proctor's version of the Avengers included alternate versions of Iron Man, Crystal, Captain America, and the Black Widow.

THE GATHERERS

As he destroyed realities, Proctor would occasionally save an Avenger from that reality and mentally manipulate them into joining him on his quest. This group of survivors were known as the Gatherers. They believed Avengers from other dimensions were responsible for their reality's destruction. When they arrived on Earth-616, their main team consisted of Mother Cassandra, the Swordsman, Magdalene, Sloth, and alternate versions of the Vision and Jocasta. Following Proctor's defeat, Magdalene and the Swordsman became honory members of the Avengers before leaving to explore other Earths.

MAD LOVE

Proctor slowly started to drive Sersi insane, but this time found himself facing the Avengers and Dane Whitman (the Black Knight). Before their final confrontation, Dane learned that Proctor was a version of himself from another reality. Dane's love for fellow Avenger Crystal prevented his psychic link with Sersi from driving him insane. During their final confrontation, Sersi killed Proctor. Her insanity was still growing and she feared she would destroy reality. The dying Watcher Ute used the last of his life-force to repair the damage done by Proctor and open a gateway to another reality for Sersi, one where she would be free of her madness. She walked through the portal, joined by Dane Whitman, and the two continued their adventures in another dimension.

During their final battle, Sersi used Proctor's own ebony blade to kill him. It was the same blade that Proctor had used to kill his version of Sersi in his own reality at the start of his madness.

THE CROSSING

The adventure known as The Crossing rocked the Avengers to its foundations. The team's lynchpin, Iron Man (Tony Stark) was revealed as a murderer and a traitor in thrall to the time-traveling Immortus. Only Tony's own 19-year-old self could thwart Immortus' world-shattering schemes. But would time, mysteriously slipping and sliding, be on the Avengers' side?

The mysterious appearance in the woods near Tony Stark's country house of a flute-playing fortune-teller calling himself Tuc was the first hint that all was not well. Tuc foretold that Marilla, the nanny to Quicksilver and Crystal's baby daughter Luna, would soon die. In reality, Tuc was Luna's brother from the future and desperate to protect his sister from a terrible fate.

MURDER MOST FOUL

Traveling through time, Yellowjacket (Rita DeMara) found herself outside Avengers Mansion—and was murdered by a shadowy, yet familiar, figure. The murder was witnessed by Luna. Later, Hank Pym, Janet Van Dyne, and Beast discovered a strange door in the lowest sub-basement of the mansion. Soon afterward, Luna's nurse Marilla was standing near this door when a figure appeared through it and murdered her. As the Avengers reeled from the shock of the two killings, another ally, the Eternal Gilgamesh, was assassinated in an upstairs room. The perpetrator escaped though the portal in the basement.

Victims of Tony Stark: Yellowjacket (right) and Marilla (below right).

TIMESLIP

Immortus was acting on the orders of the Time-Keepers who controlled the timestream. They viewed the human race, and the Avengers in particular, as a threat to their existence and convinced Immortus to do all he could to destroy Earth's Mightiest Heroes. Immortus knew that mind-controlling Tony Stark would strike at the heart of the team, while Stark's scientific skills could also be exploited. Following the murders of Yellowjacket (who had come to warn the Avengers of Immmortus' plans) and Marilla (who just happened to be in the wrong place at the wrong time), Stark tried to throw suspicion onto Hawkeye. Meanwhile, Immortus/Kang had Stark build a superweapon in his Arctic lab, designed to wipe out most of humanity. The few survivors would allegedly become super-evolved beings.

The door in the mansion's basement was a time portal and the mastermind behind the murders was Immortus, posing as Kang, who was mind-controlling Tony Stark. Among those abetting "Kang" in his everlasting mission against the Avengers and all humanity were the bloodthirsty Space Phantoms, Tobias and Malachi.

BAD MAN

The Eternal Gilgamesh had tried to warn the Avengers of Immortus' plans but had been wounded by Immortus/ Kang's Space Phantom "sons" and slain by the assassin Neut. Other warnings came intermittently from a future teenaged version of Luna, who also communicated subliminally with her much younger self. Luna's parents, Quicksilver and Crystal, thus came to suspect that their child was a murder witness—and that Tony Stark was the "bad man" she kept sobbing about. The teenaged Luna eventually arrived at Avengers Mansion. Hunted down by Neut, she revealed with her dying breath that the only person who could defeat a genius like Tony Stark was Tony Stark, his teenage self from the past.

The teenaged Luna from the future and her younger self helped alert the Avengers to Stark's treachery.

Battling an attack by Immortus' forces, the Avengers traveled back in time through their time portal to find young Tony. At first Tony was unsure what to believe. The murder of his parents by Immortus' "son" Tobias convinced him to join the Avengers. The team and young Tony were unable to follow Immortus' murdering sons through the portal. They were helped by Dr. Doom who, not wishing these Avengers to inhabit this time period, allowed them to use his time-platform. Back in their own time, the Avengers confronted their enemies. Young Tony's scientific savvy enabled himself, Masque, and Hawkeye to break into Stark's Arctic lab. A vicious battle ensued between the teenage Tony and Immortus' gang.

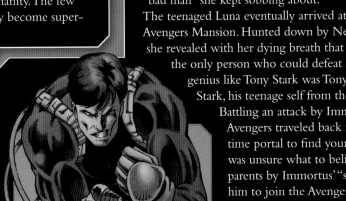

> "I'll do whatever it takes—go wherever you lead—to help you defeat these monsters!"
>
> TONY STARK, AGED 19

SACRIFICE

During the fight, young Tony was severely injured by his older self. Immortus readied his temporal transposer superweapon, planning to eliminate the Avengers and turn Earth into a "boneyard." At the last minute, Tony Stark had a moment of clarity and realized what he had done. Throwing off Immortus' influence, Tony Stark sacrificed his life to destroy the weapon and force Immortus to leave present reality. The mysterious Tuc, who had taken little Luna away to safeguard her from Immortus' crew, reappeared and delivered this epitaph: "Anthony Stark died as he always tried to live… a hero in his heart." In time, young Tony recovered from his injuries to become the new Iron Man and, with the rest of the Avengers, take on the psionic entity Onslaught.

THE AVENGERS
#400

EARTH'S MIGHTIEST HEROES
AVENGERS
JUL '96 400
GIANT-SIZE
ANNIVERSARY SPECTACULAR!
EARTH'S MIGHTIEST HEROES UP AGAINST AN ENDLESS ASSAULT OF OLD ENEMIES!

> "We've found the source of the Darkness we've been fighting—and Loki himself is the gateway!"
> **Captain America**

Main Characters: Edwin Jarvis; Tyfon the Timeskipper; Loki

Main Supporting Characters: Thor; Captain America; the Scarlet Witch; Crystal, the Vision; Quicksilver; Iron Man; Hawkeye; Giant-Man; Black Knight; Radioactive Man; Dr. Spectrum; Hyperion; Whizzer

Main Locations: Avengers Mansion; Manhattan

Publication Date
July 1996

Editor-in-chief
Bob Harras

Cover Artists
Mike Deodato Jr,
Tom Palmer

Writer
Mark Waid

Penciler
Mike Wieringo

Inker
Tom Palmer

Colorist
John Kalisz

BACKGROUND

The Avengers' 400th issue brought the title full circle with the team facing Loki, the foe who had brought them together in the first issue. Writer Mark Waid and artist Mike Wieringo teamed up for the special one-off story. Jarvis was at the center of the action, which was only fitting, as he was also the only character to have appeared in every Avengers lineup (albeit as an auxiliary helper rather than superpowered member). The next issue saw the start of the Onslaught saga, leading to the cancellation of the title and the team's rebirth in a new *Avengers* title by Rob Liefeld and Jim Valentino.

Jarvis was sweeping up the leaves in the grounds of Avengers Mansion when Tyfon the Timeskipper materialized. In great agitation, Tyfon declared that the Avengers were doomed to die that very day and only Jarvis could save them **(1)**.

The Avengers, meanwhile, were in Manhattan combating the Black Knight and Radioactive Man to great acclaim. The cheering stopped when the villains mysteriously disappeared in a shadowy substance that also engulfed several skyscrapers **(2)**.

Back at the mansion, Tyfon told Jarvis that, in addition to the death threat hanging over the Avengers, the heroes' greatest foe was about to plunge the planet into a "monstrous darkness that will plague all future generations." Once the villain was identified, he could be stopped. But who was he? Jarvis, with his encyclopedic knowledge of the Avengers' exploits must know…

Tyfon investigated Jarvis' memories using a machine that visualized them onscreen. At the same time, Tyfon was monitoring events downtown. Somehow the Avengers' past was being used against them. The team members were fighting a legion of past enemies **(3)**. Outnumbered, exhausted,

The Story

It had been foretold that on this day the Avengers' greatest foe would open up a vast dimensional portal linking everyday reality to a dark dimension. The only way to stop this apocalyptic event was to discover the identity of the Avengers' greatest enemy, a foe capable of recreating a rogues gallery of Super Villains from the past, and defeat him.

"Edwin Jarvis… today is the day the Avengers die… and only you can save them!"

Tyfon the Timeskipper to Jarvis

one by one, the Avengers were falling as the Darkness, a form of "organic proto-matter," swallowed up the city.

Jarvis racked his brains to figure out who could have unleashed the Darkness. Then he recalled the Avengers' very first mission— battling the wiles of a certain Norse trickster god… As soon as Jarvis uttered the name "Loki," the villain himself appeared, boasting of his coming triumph, and hurling Jarvis aside **(4)**. Jarvis used his special ID card to summon the Avengers.

United once more, Earth's Mightiest Heroes confronted Loki. The trickster responded by creating his own army—the Avengers' statues coated in Adamantium. The Scarlet Witch melted the animated statues with her hex power, but they combined into an Adamantium wave that threatened to engulf the Avengers. Thor's whirling hammer turned the wave back onto Loki, turning him into a living statue **(5)**, and simultaneously closing the gateway (Loki himself) to shut out the Darkness.

The world was safe once more, but the Avengers had no time to celebrate. Nate Grey of the X-Men showed up to announce a new crisis: Professor X had gone insane!

ONSLAUGHT

Quicksilver rashly attacked Joseph, believing him to be a rejuvenated version of Magneto and responsible for Xavier attacking the X-Men.

Onslaught was the darkness Charles Xavier had kept trapped in his mind combined with the desire for vengeance that dominated Magneto. When Xavier used his powers to close down his friend's mind, the darkness from both men took on a physical form—Onslaught!

THE BATTLE BEGINS

Captain America revealed his tactical acumen by getting Holocaust to attack Post, helping the Avengers win the battle against the two powerful mutants.

Once Onslaught gained physical form, he manipulated events from a distance. When the Avengers found Xavier standing over the bodies of the X-Men, they believed the X-Men's leader had fallen under Magneto's control. The truth was far worse. Xavier was trapped inside Onslaught (together with Nate Grey and Franklin Richards) and being used to increase Onslaught's already formidable psychic powers. After realizing the man known as Joseph wasn't the same Magneto they had once feared, the Avengers tried to save New York from attack by Onslaught's acolytes Post and Holocaust. The Avengers were outmatched until Captain America tricked Holocaust into attacking Post, removing one enemy from the fight. The Avengers then threw all their might against Holocaust, defeating the villain. But one enemy remained: the Avengers had to face Onslaught.

The X-Men, Fantastic Four, Avengers, Hulk, and other heroes joined forces for the final confrontation with Onslaught. The battle took place in Central Park and resulted in the Avengers and Fantastic Four vanishing from Earth to an alternative pocket universe.

"I have no use for humanity!" ONSLAUGHT

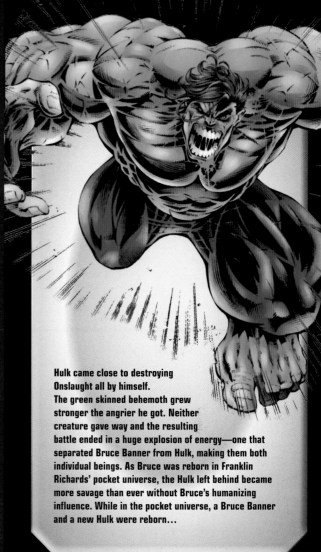

Hulk came close to destroying Onslaught all by himself. The green skinned behemoth grew stronger the angrier he got. Neither creature gave way and the resulting battle ended in a huge explosion of energy—one that separated Bruce Banner from Hulk, making them both individual beings. As Bruce was reborn in Franklin Richards' pocket universe, the Hulk left behind became more savage than ever without Bruce's humanizing influence. While in the pocket universe, a Bruce Banner and a new Hulk were reborn...

THE LAST BATTLE

Onslaught wanted to enslave humanity, but was faced with opposition from a host of Super Heroes. The final battle took place in Central Park with a rampaging Hulk the first to strike. Hulk fought with a fury rarely seen, growing stronger the more Onslaught angered him. There was a vast explosion and it looked like Onslaught was down. Nearby lay Bruce Banner and the Hulk, separated at last. Onslaught recovered, the mutant had already evolved into a being of pure energy. The only hope was to contain Onslaught, now a swirling vortex of power threatening reality itself. Thor rushed headlong into the vortex, draining some of Onslaught's power. The other heroes soon followed. Only mutants were forced to hold back as their powers would only have helped their enemy recover. The Thing and Human Torch entered, shortly followed by Captain America and the Avengers. The heroes knew it might be their last act but also knew it was the only chance the world had of being spared Onslaught's wrath. As Reed and Sue Richards entered, Reed told the X-Men to blast the weakened Onslaught with everything they had. As Onslaught started to destabilize, Bruce Banner became the last hero to disappear. Inside Onslaught, Xavier, Nate, and Franklin managed to break free moments before Onslaught exploded. The threat was at an end and Onslaught was no more.

Once Onslaught's armor was destroyed, he became pure psychic energy.

SAVED

The heroes who entered the Onslaught energy being were gone. Franklin Richards had lost his parents to Onslaught. Only later was it revealed that Franklin had saved his family and friends, building a brave new world for them. One on which the Fantastic Four and Avengers were reborn...

Loki was reborn with the heroes. He again planned Thor's destruction and sought control of an Earth that lacked Odin's protection.

REBORN

Kang was once again one of the first enemies to face the Avengers. The time-traveling despot tried to capture the team and use it as a trophy to impress Mantis. The Avengers escaped and defeated Kang but the Swordsman was left with the strange feeling that he had met Mantis before...

Following their sacrifice against Onslaught, the Avengers were reborn in another universe. At first they had no memory of their previous incarnation but as time passed, echoes started to return...

A NEW WORLD

Loki had been reborn with the heroes into a new universe. Sensing Asgard and Odin were no longer in existence, Loki launched a fresh attack on Thor. Unknown to Loki, the Avengers had already formed on Earth. When archeologist Donald Blake found the body of Thor frozen in a bloke of ice, the Avengers were called in to investigate. The team was made up of Captain America, Iron Man, Hawkeye, the Vision, the Scarlet Witch, Hellcat, and the Swordsman, each with different origins and histories than their previous incarnations. Loki used his power to trick Thor into attacking the team but the heroes soon joined forces against the trickster. The Avengers found themselves facing new versions of the Lethal Legion and the Masters of Evil. When the Vision was damaged, Ant-Man shrunk to a microscopic size to fix his ally (something he had done before on the Earth-616 of the original Avengers team) and he had a strange sense of déjà vu. The Avengers and the Fantastic Four were brought together to face the threat of Galactus, the eater of worlds. In this reality Galactus had four heralds—including the Silver Surfer. Dr. Doom helped the heroes save the world, traveling back in time to do so but many of the heroes had started to sense something was wrong, that something important was missing...

The Enchantress plotted with Loki.

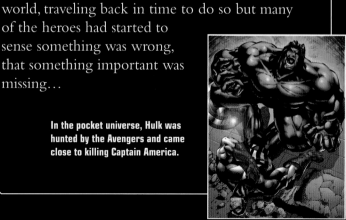

In the pocket universe, Hulk was hunted by the Avengers and came close to killing Captain America.

WORLDS COLLIDE

Franklin Richards had used his vast powers to create the pocket universe that had been home to the Avengers and other heroes for a year. The vast use of power had brought Franklin to the attention of the powerful Celestials, who sent an emissary, Ashema, to Franklin. Ashema gave the boy a stark choice: only one of the realities would be able to survive and Franklin had to choose which one. The boy was terrified and fled into the pocket universe to ask his parents for help. While they didn't recognize him at first, his appearance reawakened Sue Richards' memories. Reed and Iron Man soon learned that Franklin was speaking the truth—their Earth is only a year old! Ashema gained humanity after restoring an injured Franklin to health but her fellow Celestials decided to destroy the Counter Earth.

Franklin Richards had created a pocket universe to save all the heroes who had fought Onslaught—including his parents.

Thanks to an interdimensional spaceship created by Victor Von Doom, the heroes were able to break through from the pocket universe to their own reality.

Thor and Mr. Fantastic fought to stop Doom claiming Franklin's cosmic power.

THE RETURN

Salvation came in the form of a ship created by Dr. Doom to return them home. The heroes convinced Ashema to allow both realities to survive. As they traveled through the dimensional barrier between worlds, Doom attempted to steal Franklin's power for himself. Reed and Thor managed to stop him, Thor vanishing with the villain into a dimensional rift. As they reached their home reality, memories of their previous lives came rushing back. The heroes had returned…

THE DESTINY WAR

It was a conflict that stretched across time as Rick Jones brought together a unique team of Avengers to save humanity and prevent the Time-Keepers from committing chronal genocide...

RICK JONES

Rick Jones had manifested the Destiny Force during the Kree-Skrull War, creating numerous timelines. Because of this, the Time-Keepers believed that all humans would one day be able to access the powerful Force. Fortunately, the Destiny Force allowed Jones to unwittingly select members of the Avengers from various points in time who would best help him defeat the Time-Keepers.

CONFLICT IN TIME

When Immortus sent his agent Tempus to kill Rick Jones, it signaled the start of the Destiny War. Jones, at the time crippled, was saved by Kang, the villain Libra, and the Kree's Supreme Intelligence. They helped Jones access the powerful Destiny Force (which Jones had used during the Kree-Skrull War) to pull seven Avengers out of time to aid him. Immortus had gained possession of the Time Crystal, a powerful artifact that could control realities. The Avengers fought Immortus across time, their very existence at stake.

The War brought Kang and Immortus into conflict again. Immortus was a future version of Kang but Kang constantly fought to avoid becoming his future self.

AVENGERS FOREVER

Rick Jones brought together present day Avengers Giant-Man and the Wasp with several Avengers from other eras. Captain America came from when he was traumatized by the Secret Empire's corruption of the White House; Hawkeye from early in his career when he was more aggressive; and Yellowjacket from his wedding day (when he was in a delusional state), while Captain Marvel (Genis–Vell) and Songbird were pulled from future incarnations of the Avengers. Each hero would fulfill a specific role in the epic adventure that followed.

SPACE PHANTOM

The Space Phantom was one of the first foes the Avengers ever faced. During the Destiny War the Avengers learned that there was not just one Space Phantom but a whole race. They lived in limbo and served Immortus. Space Phantoms can change themselves into a perfect duplicate of someone. The person they copy is then sent to limbo while the Space Phantom has their form. Space Phantoms were used by Immortus in a number of attempts to disrupt or destroy the Avengers.

AVENGERS BATALLION

In many realities, humanity had created a Terran Empire—with the Avengers leading humanity's brutal conquest of alien worlds. The Time-Keepers decided to wipe out humanity from a number of realities using a Chrono-Cannon powered by the Forever Crystal. They also pulled evil versions of the Avengers from out of the timestream to stop Jones' team from damaging their plans.

Yellowjacket betrayed the Avengers to Immortus. On learning of Immortus' plans to wipe out humanity, he swapped sides again.

TIME-KEEPERS

The Time-Keepers had been created by the last surviving member of the Time Variance Authority (a group that watched over time and space) at the end of the Universe. They ordered Immortus to wipe out the Avengers but instead Immortus tried to guide the team's actions. The Time-Keepers eventually killed Immortus and tried to bring Kang to their side by speeding up his evolution into Immortus. Their plan failed and they only succeeded in separating Immortus from Kang—creating two completely separate beings.

FINAL BATTLE

Rick Jones, working with a future incarnation of himself, used the Destiny Force to summon more Avengers to fight Immortus's evil forces. The conflict ended when Captain America shattered the Forever Crystal. Rick Jones nearly died destroying the Chrono-Cannon but was saved by bonding with Captain Marvel. The Avengers were then returned to their respective time periods.

THE AVENGERS #1 (1998)

"This seems overdue, somehow—we've been back for a while, but it took this... situation... to bring us together."
The Wasp

Main Characters: Captain America; Iron Man; Thor; Giant-Man; the Wasp; Hawkeye; Quicksilver; the Scarlet Witch

Main Supporting Characters: Jarvis; Rick Jones; D-Man; Crystal; Quasar; Hercules

Main Locations: New York City; Avengers Mansion; Asgard; Tintagel Head

Publication Date
February 1998

Editor in Chief
Bob Harras

Cover Artists
George Pérez,
Tom Smith

Writer
Kurt Busiek

Penciler
George Pérez

Inker
Al Vey

Colorist
Tom Smith

BACKGROUND

Onslaught killed Earth's Mightiest Heroes. *Heroes Reborn* resurrected them. But it took the efforts of two fan-favorite comic book creators to relaunch Marvel Comics' seminal super-team title with all the anticipated energy and creativity to meet readers' expectations of what a comic book like *The Avengers* should deliver month after month. And deliver it did, as writer Kurt Busiek and artist George Pérez reassembled Earth's Mightiest Heroes to face an obscure old foe with deadly new plans for world domination!

HISTORY LESSON

Initially, Marvel wanted Pérez to write and draw *The Avengers* himself. But the accomplished artist instead called upon Busiek, a creator he longed to work with, to collaborate with him in restoring Earth's Mightiest Heroes to greatness. Busiek brought with him an unparalleled knowledge of Marvel lore, while Pérez— who had drawn the title to much acclaim in the 1970s and 1980s—was able to fill every nook and cranny of the page with practically every hero and heroine who had ever ever been an Avenger! But at the heart of it, both Busiek and Pérez realized that the classic core team of Earth's Mightiest Heroes was instrumental to their success, as evidenced by the opening splash page featuring a gilded statue of six stalwart teammates, heralding a new Golden Age in Avengers storytelling!

ONCE AN AVENGER...

The Story

The Avengers had weathered far worse, but as Captain America, Iron Man, and the Wasp convened at Avengers Mansion to discuss the future of Earth's Mightiest Heroes, a storm raged outside and all around the world as nearly every past member of the team confronted monstrous threats of unknown origin!

To each Avenger—including Bonita Juarez (Firebird)—the arcane attacks seemed random, with mystical creatures rising up to confront them wherever they lived **(1)**! Only after assembling at the Avengers' Fifth Avenue townhouse and comparing notes did Earth's Mightiest Heroes realize that each had battled menaces from Norse mythology **(2)**. These were not isolated incidents—but targeted strikes from a common threat! Thor confirmed these suspicions when he arrived at Avengers HQ after a harrowing journey through a destroyed Asgard. There, Thor found the home of the Norse Gods deserted and cut off from the other Nine Realms following the destruction of the rainbow bridge **(3)**. Thor's worst fear was realized when he discovered the Twilight Sword, Agard's most powerful and dangerous weapon, was missing! The Twilight Sword had the power to destroy or remake creation according to the whim of whoever wielded it together with the fabled Norn Stones—which Thor sensed were lost somewhere in Midgard, the realm of mankind.

Aboard five identical Quinjets, the Avengers flew around the world in search of the

> "Once more then, the word must be spread, and the battle-clarion must be sounded. In every corner of Midgard... let the cry ring out— AVENGERS ASSEMBLE!"
>
> Thor

Sword and the Stones **(4)**. High above Tintagel Head, off the coast of Cornwall, England, one of the Quinjets was nearly knocked out of the sky by a freak whirlwind conjured up by Mordred the Evil **(5)**. Earth's Mightiest Heroes soon discovered that Mordred was merely a pawn in the evil schemes of his aunt, Morgan Le Fay, a former foe of the Avengers **(6)**. As the other Avengers teams faced Le Fay's mythological minions around the world, the sinister sorceress revealed that her attacks were part of a ruse to cause Earth's Mightiest Heroes to regroup. She hoped the Avengers would unwittingly deliver the Scarlet Witch **(7)**, the one teammate whose chaos magicks would bridge the gap between La Fay's Celtic sorcery and the Asgardian powers, allowing her to wield the Twilight Sword. With the sword in her grasp, Le Fay remade reality according to her own diabolical designs. The newly reformed Avengers, Earth's Mightiest Heroes in any time or place, had their work cut out for them...

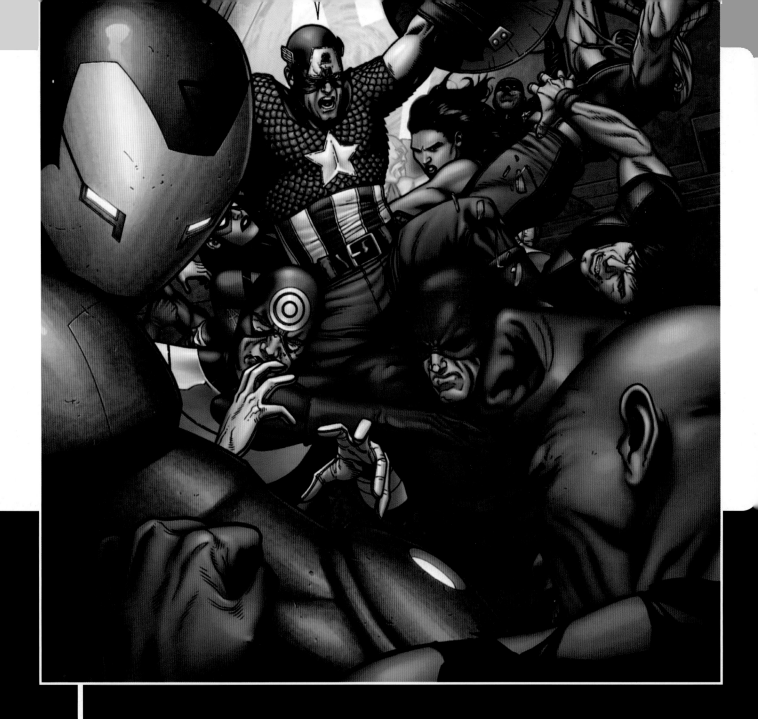

the **2000s**

A new millennium brought major change to Earth's Mightiest Heroes. For a while, the rallying cry—"Avengers Assemble!"—would be heard no more as the team disassembled, destroyed from within by the Scarlet Witch!

Believing the Avengers to blame for the loss of her children, the Scarlet Witch used her hex powers to initiate seemingly random attacks on Earth's Mightiest Heroes. Thus, Marvel deconstructed its premier super-team beginning in *Avengers: Disassembled*, closely followed by the introduction of a world stripped of mutantkind in *House of M*. Though the Avengers would quickly reassemble in the wake of these Earth-shaking events, the Marvel Universe was headed for even more groundbreaking changes that would redefine the roles of Super Heroes for both the publisher and the genre. *Civil War* turned friend against friend and established a new status quo for costumed champions in a paranoid post-9/11 world. And as readers raced to keep up with the changing face of the Marvel Universe, a full-scale Secret Invasion from the shapeshifting Skrulls would reveal that no hero, villain, or supporting character could be trusted!

OVERLEAF

Would-be master of the universe Korvac would return to battle more than one Avengers team. But, as in all his previous attempts to remake reality, the mad man-god would face defeat at the hands of Earth's Mightiest Heroes.

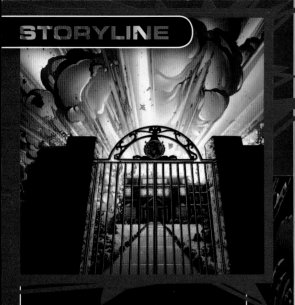

Avengers Disassembled

The Avengers team fragmented when the Scarlet Witch's mind fragmented. She unleashed the full measure of her mutant "chaos magicks" upon the team that she had served for years, vengefully disassembling Earth's Mightiest Heroes as she slipped into madness...

SUDDEN DEATH

For years, the Scarlet Witch had wielded her hex powers for the good of mankind—but no longer. Chaos ruled her troubled psyche, and Wanda Maximoff loosed her magicks upon the unsuspecting Avengers. Former teammate Jack of Hearts—previously killed in action—somehow returned to life as a walking corpse, breached the security of Avengers Mansion, and killed Ant-Man Scott Lang— as well as razing nearly half of the team's headquarters! Later, Tony Stark stood before the United Nations and inexplicably berated the Latverian delegate in a drunken tirade, though he had not taken a drink in years. And as the stunned Avengers gazed at the smoldering ruins of Avengers Mansion, the Vision crashed a Quinjet almost at their feet before disgorging an army of Ultrons from inside his synthezoid body!

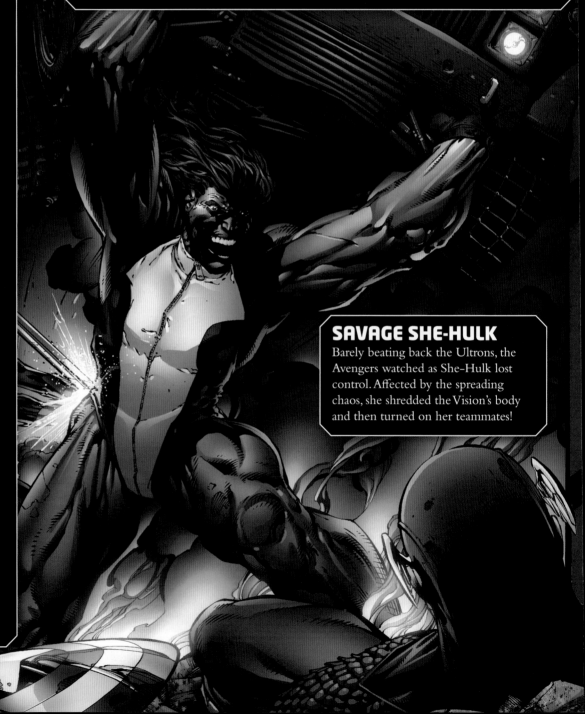

SAVAGE SHE-HULK

Barely beating back the Ultrons, the Avengers watched as She-Hulk lost control. Affected by the spreading chaos, she shredded the Vision's body and then turned on her teammates!

Answering the call to assemble, every living Avenger, past or present, gathered at the wreckage of Avengers Mansion to discover that one of their own had betrayed them!

CHAOS RULES

The Scarlet Witch was driven to madness by the loss of her children, who were themselves magical constructs she had subconsciously "created." Wanda blamed the Avengers for her loss. Every subsequent use of her chaos magicks made tiny warps in reality that eventually unwound the fragile fabric of her sanity. In her own newly constructed reality, Wanda's twin boys lived once more, but she feared that Earth's Mightiest Heroes would take her children again. So she unleashed chaos against the Avengers, the team that, ironically, had been Wanda's one true family for most of her life.

Before Earth's Mightiest Heroes could stop the Scarlet Witch, more chaos ensued as an armada of Kree warships materialized in the skies over New York!

> "Drama, conflict, tragedy. They become excuses to change the world to fit the image that she has for it."
>
> DR. STRANGE

Dr. Strange diagnosed Wanda's malady: a chaos-fueled madness that stemmed from a series of tragedies, both real and imagined. In the end, Wanda's father, Magneto, spirited the unconscious Wanda away to the ruins of Genosha where he hoped to help her heal...

AVENGERS NO MORE

Though the Scarlet Witch had been subdued, the damage she had inflicted upon the Avengers was irreparable. Tony Stark's apparent drunken outburst at the U.N. had undermined his financial standing. He could no longer fund his failing company and Earth's Mightiest Heroes. Without the Maria Stark Foundation, and having no headquarters to call home, the team decided it had no choice but to disband for now, following a few happy recollections of the team's former glory days.

THE AVENGERS

#503

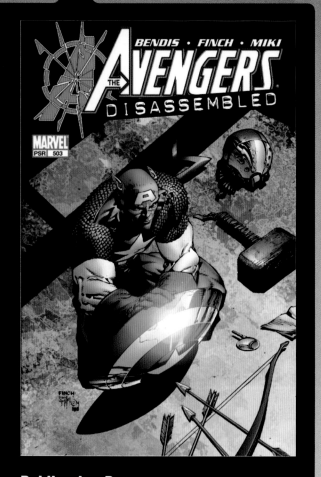

*"Where are my children?
Tell me where my children are!"*
The Scarlet Witch

Main Characters: The Scarlet Witch; Dr. Strange
Main Supporting Characters: Captain America,
Iron Man; Agatha Harkness; Magneto
Main Location: The grounds of Avengers Mansion

Publication Date
November 2004

Editor-in-Chief
Joe Quesada

Cover Artists
David Finch, Danny Miki

Writer
Brian Michael Bendis

Pencilers
David Finch, Olivier Coipel

Inker
Danny Miki

Colorist
Frank D'Armata

BACKGROUND

The 500th issue of *The Avengers* was always going to be something special. Volume Three of the series had reached 84 issues before it returned to its original numbering for the anniversary issue. Writer Brian Michael Bendis came on board, accompanied by artist David Finch, and proceeded to shake the foundations of the Avengers with the four-part "Chaos" epic. Under the stewardship of Editor-in-Chief Joe Quesada, Marvel was undergoing a renaissance, partly due to the quality of creators Quesada was bringing in to the company. Bendis was at the forefront of the new talent and had been at the helm of the exceptionally successful *Ultimate Spider-Man* series (released in 2000). In the space of four issues, he tore the Avengers apart, killing several popular members and ending the title with the team disassembled. It set the scene for a new title: *The New Avengers*, as Bendis and Finch gave Marvel's mightiest heroes a bold new direction and placed them at the center of the Marvel Universe for years to come...

The Story

The Avengers were on Code White, the highest-level emergency, having endured a sequence of inexplicable, vicious attacks. Dr. Strange revealed that magic was at the root of recent events. But who was responsible for this orgy of malign spell-casting? And what could they want?

Then: Janet Van Dyne (the Wasp) and Wanda Maximoff (the Scarlet Witch), were relaxing in the grounds of Avengers Mansion. Jan touched on the topic of having children (1), sparking a hostile reaction…

Now: The Avengers assembled in the grounds of the now-ruined mansion hoping that the mage Dr. Strange could shed light on the recent mayhem. Strange asked whether there was anyone among the Avengers' ranks capable of orchestrating this level of chaos.

> ### "You will stop this madness. These magicks are not yours to abuse."
>
> Dr. Strange to the Scarlet Witch

Then: Wanda paid a visit to her erstwhile mentor, the witch Agatha Harkness (2). Jan's remark had awakened a buried memory. Wanda had questions for Agatha concerning two missing children…

Now: The Avengers debated Strange's question, and Wanda's name came up. They recalled that she once magically conjured up two children, but that Agatha Harkness had "erased" them, along with Wanda's memory of having had them. Strange maintained that losing her "children" had driven Wanda insane; she was responsible for the crisis. Captain America, who had developed strong feelings for Wanda, discovered her serving dinner to her phantom children (3). She used magic to drive him away and accused the Avengers of conspiring to take her "children."

Insane, vengeful Wanda confronted the Avengers (4) and conjured up magical versions of their worst foes (5). Dr. Strange broke her spell (6), and Captain America caught her unconscious body as it fell (7). Wanda's father, Magneto, then took custody of his daughter and flew off with her, pursued by the Avengers. Meanwhile, Colonel Nick Fury came upon Agatha Harkness' corpse. She had clearly been dead for some time.

A seemingly random gathering of heroes during a moment of crisis led to the formation of an all-new team of Avengers!

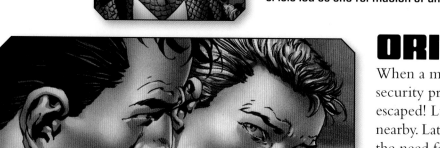

ORIGINS

When a mass breakout occurred at the maximum-security prison known as the Raft, 87 Super Villains escaped! Luckily, a small contingent of heroes were nearby. Later, Tony Stark and Steve Rogers realized the need for an able team of Avengers to deal with such threats. Although SHIELD was reluctant to endorse a new force of Earth's Mightiest Heroes, Cap reminded the agency that his "Full Champion License" gave him official sanction to assemble any team he required for any mission, including this one.

STARK TOWER

At Tony Stark's strong suggestion, the new team of Avengers established its headquarters at Stark Tower. The gleaming edifice located ten blocks away from the Fantastic Four's Baxter Building made the perfect base. Earth's Mightiest Heroes occupied the top three floors of the structure, situated right in the heart of Manhattan. In addition to the advanced training facilities, meeting areas, and residences for members (see pages 52–53), Stark Tower is also prime real estate for the team that has called the Big Apple its home since its original formation.

FIRST ORDER OF BUSINESS

If the events at the Raft were the new Avengers' trial by fire, the fledgling team was further tested by having to round up nearly 40 remaining escaped Super Villains, none of whom were eager to return to prison. The Avengers' first order of business was to track down and capture the mutant Karl Lykos (Sauron), whose liberation was plotted by a group calling itself the Savage Land Mutates.

THE NEW AVENGERS

Captain America's new team of Avengers initially included all of the heroes who had fought to contain the Raft jailbreak. In addition to Cap, the roster included founding Avenger Iron Man, Spider-Man, Sentry, Spider-Woman, Wolverine, and Luke Cage. Daredevil declined membership at first, instead recommending the enigmatic Ronin to take his place.

CONSPIRACY

The Avengers knew that it was Electro who had ignited the massive explosion that freed the Raft's Super Villain prisoners. But the team was soon to discover that the electrically-powered criminal had been paid to cause the jailbreak so that Sauron could escape in the confusion that followed. Tracking the evil mutant to the Savage Land, an unspoiled jungle region still populated by dinosaurs, the Avengers discovered a hero who would join their ranks, as well as a shocking conspiracy involving SHIELD itself!

Sauron and the Savage Land Mutates were involved with an illegal Vibranium mining operation using slave labor. Much to the heroes' dismay, a rogue faction of SHIELD was linked to the scheme!

The X-Men joined forces with the Avengers, helping to fend off dinosaurs and dismantle the mining operation. Wolverine was invited to join the Avengers, with the proviso that he could remain an active member of the X-Men as well.

This Avengers team placed no restrictions on membership or active duty, preferring instead a more fluid roster that allowed for teammates to be called upon as necessity dictated. Any Avenger past or present is welcome at meetings atop Stark Tower.

THE NEW AVENGERS
Vol.1 #1

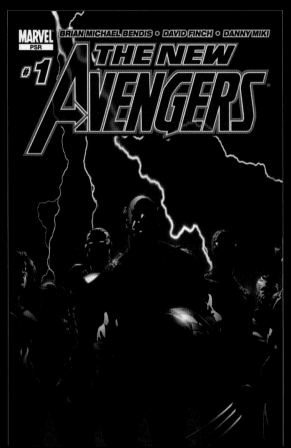

"The Avengers called it quits. We believe the time is now."
Anonymous

Main Characters: Captain America; Spider-Man; Jessica Drew; Matt Murdock; Luke Cage
Main Supporting Characters: Foggy Nelson; Sentry
Main Locations: New York City; the Raft

Publication Date
December 2004

Editor in Chief
Joe Quesada

Cover Artists
David Finch,
Danny Miki

Writer
Brian Michael Bendis

Penciler
David Finch

Inker
Danny Miki

Colorist
Frank
D'Armata

BACKGROUND

By the 21st century, the Avengers were an institution in the Marvel Universe. However, following the harrowing "Avengers Disassembled" storyline, the future was uncertain for Earth's Mightiest Heroes. The news was sad but true: the Avengers had disbanded. With the launch of *The New Avengers* #1, Brian Michael Bendis and David Finch (who had previously worked on *X-Men* and *The Avengers*) rebooted the franchise with a little shock therapy courtesy of Electro and a massive Super Villain prison break. The team is not referred to as the "New" Avengers within the series because, Bendis has said, its members believe they are the only authentic Avengers team (as opposed to the government-sanctioned Mighty Avengers who later had their own series). *The New Avengers* saw the bringing together of a somewhat unlikely grouping of Avengers both old and new.

The Story

"Breakout! Part One" started with Electro accepting a job from shady benefactors who believed that no New York-based Super Hero group would stop their secret plans. The Avengers began with a handful of solo heroes in the right place at the wrong time. A bolt of lightning would herald a repeat of history...

2

> "My name is Max Dillon. Some of you know me, some of you don't—but I broke you losers out! Have fun, enjoy your lives... but from here on in, now and forever... you guys owe me HUGE!"
>
> Electro

3

4

The setting was the Raft, a maximum-maximum Super Villain prison atoll adjacent to Ryker's Island Prison in New York City's East River. Arriving at the SHIELD-run facility to visit a new and powerful inmate for reasons **1** soon to be revealed, lawyers Matt Murdock and Foggy Nelson, plus their hired muscle Luke Cage, got the grand tour courtesy of SHIELD's Jessica Drew **(1)**. Little did any of them know that Electro would soon strike, killing the Raft's power grid before lighting up the prison with devastating electrical blasts that freed its population of 87 super-prisoners **(2)**, including some of the worst and most unrepentant villains on Earth **(3)**.

Electro's lightning show drew the attention of both Captain America and Spider-Man, the latter hitching a ride on Cap's SHIELD helicopter before an errant jolt of electricity brought it crashing down in flames **(4)**! Undeterred, the heroes made their way into the prison, only to face an overwhelming force, as villains incarcerated by both heroes—and the mighty Avengers—attacked with murder on their minds!

Meanwhile, in the bowels of the super-penitentiary, Murdock, Nelson, Cage, and Drew did their best to remain alive. Luckily, three of the four had experience as Super Heroes themselves! Murdock was a man without fear, the costumed Daredevil, until his identity was revealed to the public, though he denied the charge. Cage was known familiarly as Power Man, a hero-for-hire. And Jessica Drew was the first Spider-Woman. Things looked grim until the quartet found the man they had come to visit, the disgraced hero Sentry, imprisoned for killing his wife **(5)**. Once missing in action for decades, and very likely the most powerful superhuman on the planet, Sentry might be their only hope. A bold new lineup of Avengers was already taking shape.

5

Although vastly outnumbered by Super Villains, the New Avengers seemed the best bet as Earth's Mightiest Heroes began an epic adventure that began on a sinking "Raft" and ended in the dinosaur inhabited Savage Land!

139

SPIDER-WOMAN

Jessica Drew's intelligence and spidery superpowers were first put to use by HYDRA. But Jessica rebelled against the criminal group, joined SHIELD, and eventually became a member of the Avengers.

Like Spider-Man, who gained his abilities similarly, Jessica can climb virtually any surface and hang from walls or ceilings, stuck fast like an agile spider. These powers make her uniquely qualified in missions involving stealth and espionage.

Spider-Woman learned various fighting styles under the tutelage of the Taskmaster, including judo, boxing, and capoeira.

Oh, What A Tangled Web...

In her debut, Spider-Woman was caught up in a web of deceit as a pawn of HYDRA.

As a child, Jessica Drew suffered uranium poisoning. To save her, her geneticist father Jonathan injected her with irradiated spider's blood. When that failed, Jonathan placed her in a genetic accelerator chamber belonging to his colleague Herbert Wyndham (the High Evolutionary) to speed up the process. But Jessica lay in the chamber for decades after her parents and the High Evolutionary mysteriously disappeared. Jessica only realized later that the process imbued her with superpowers, largely due to the spider's blood now fused to her at the molecular level. Unsure of who she was or what she had become, Jessica became an unwitting pawn of Otto Vermis, a leader of HYDRA, who dispatched Jessica as Spider-Woman to assassinate Nick Fury of SHIELD. Instead, Jessica began working for Fury. Much later, Jessica served SHIELD as a liaison to the Super Villain prison known as the Raft. Following a massive jailbreak, Jessica became part of a new team of Avengers, though the team later discovered that this Spider-Woman was,

A chance encounter with Spider-Man encouraged Jessica to use her abilities to help others, both in-costume and as a private investigator.

Jessica's scent can elicit sexual attraction. It is uncertain whether or not these pheromones caused her romantic entanglement with Tony Stark, or whether it was mere mutual attraction.

The High Evolutionary's genetic accelerator gave Jessica incredible powers!

in fact, Skrull Queen Veranke hoping to infiltrate the Avengers. Iron Man freed the real Jessica Drew from Skrull captivity and she soon joined the Avengers for real. She also became an agent of SWORD to investigate extraterrestrial threats on Earth.

After Spider-Woman tried and failed to kill Nick Fury, the SHIELD director convinced Jessica to work as a triple agent and spy on HYDRA!

Though the Spider-Woman who joined the most recent incarnation of the Avengers was really a Skrull in disguise, Jessica herself later joined the team, anxious to undo the damage to her reputation—and to fight HYDRA once more.

Jessica gives off unique pheromones that attract men and repulse other females.

Spider-Woman recently acquired the ability to fly, though she has kept her costume's collapsible wings.

"FRANKLY, YOU DON'T KNOW HOW MUCH TROUBLE YOU'RE IN. I'LL GIVE YOU A HINT: IT'S A LOT."

KEY DATA

REAL NAME Jessica Drew

OCCUPATION Adventurer, private investigator

AFFILIATIONS The Avengers, SWORD

POWERS/WEAPONS Spider-Woman possesses superhuman strength, speed, and agility. She is able to adhere to any surface, spider-like, thanks to secretions from the palms of her hands and soles of her feet. She can also generate jolting bioelectric stings of varying intensity.

KISS OF THE SPIDER-WOMAN
Spider-Woman's "venom blasts" are actually jolts of bioelectric energy that can stun or even kill opponents if sufficiently focused.

Because she was one of the unlucky heroes and heroines captured and impersonated by Skrulls during the Secret Invasion, Spider-Woman also serves as an agent of SWORD as a fully sanctioned alien hunter.

LUKE CAGE "SWEET CHRISTMAS!"

The Avengers are known for offering ex-criminals a second chance. Luke Cage, once known as Power Man, is no different... except he was framed for a crime he didn't commit and acquired his superhuman abilities in jail!

Hero for Hire

Luke Cage started out as a "hero for hire"—with varying degrees of success.

Carl Lucas grew up on the mean streets of Harlem, running with criminal gangs alongside his boyhood friend Willis Stryker. Lucas realized that his illegal actions were hurting his family and worked to free himself from that life. Unfortunately, Stryker planted heroin in Carl's apartment, and Lucas was framed and jailed for drug possession.

In Seagate Prison, Lucas volunteered to become a test subject for Dr. Noah Burstein's cell regeneration experiments using a variation on the Super Soldier Serum that had once turned a weakling Steve Rogers into Captain America. But a vengeful guard flooded Lucas' body with an excessive amount of the serum. The already heavily muscled Carl Lucas became virtually bulletproof and superstrong.

Made nearly unbreakable, Lucas used his new abilities to escape from Seagate and make his way back to New York, where he decided to use his powers for profit, renaming himself Luke Cage, Hero for Hire, a superhuman who charged billable hours for his services. Later, Danny Rand, the martial artist known as Iron Fist joined Cage, and the firm became Heroes for Hire. Not always motivated by his earning potential, Luke Cage served as a member of the Defenders and the Fantastic Four, before he joined the Avengers following the Super Villain jailbreak at the Raft prison.

When Norman Osborn was expelled from HAMMER, Cage was given leadership of a new Avengers team by Captain America. Cage's group had carte blanche to operate below the government radar and target evildoers using methods as down and dirty as one would expect from a former street fighting man.

Luke is married to Jessica Jones (Jewel). They have an adorable baby daughter who gets a lot of attention from their Avengers' teammates.

Iron Fist has fought alongside Luke Cage for years, since their Heroes for Hire business. They joined the Avengers at the same time.

Unlike the more public team of Avengers based in Stark Tower, Luke Cage's team was given free rein to protect the world any way they saw fit.

The only problem with having impenetrable skin is that it makes treating Luke Cage's infrequent internal injuries next to impossible without the aid of high-powered medical lasers or Adamantium surgical instruments.

Luke ran his Avengers team out of the old Avengers Mansion, which he purchased from Tony Stark for the measly sum of one dollar... which Iron Fist had loaned him.

KEY DATA

REAL NAME Carl Lucas

OCCUPATION Adventurer

AFFILIATIONS The Avengers, the Thunderbolts, the Fantastic Four, Heroes for Hire, the Defenders

POWERS/WEAPONS Luke Cage possesses steel-hard skin and superstrength, as well as a superhuman capacity to heal quickly from most grievous injuries.

Luke studied law in prison and knows several languages. He is a charismatic orator, known for speaking the plain truth even if it hurts.

Luke's impenetrable skin is bulletproof and resistant to electrical charges and extremes in temperature.

Luke's invulnerability does not extend to his clothing, which is often left in tatters.

POSSESSED
Shortly after Luke was given charge of an Avengers team, he was possessed by Agamotto, who was attempting to reclaim the magical amulet "the Eye of Agamotto" from Earth's Sorcerer Supreme. The threat was ended by Dr. Voodoo.

"THIS AIN'T HIS AVENGERS, THIS IS *MY* AVENGERS... TRY IT OUT. DON'T SAY NO."

Presently, Luke Cage is leader of the Thunderbolts Program, now officially sanctioned by Steve Rogers. The program offers reformed super-criminals a chance at redemption by behaving responsibly and using their abilities for good, as the former Power Man once did.

WOLVERINE

"I'M THE BEST THERE IS AT WHAT I DO, BUT WHAT I DO ISN'T VERY NICE."

Wolverine is a dangerous mutant. He is a feral fighter who, despite being a loner at heart, divides his time between fighting with the Avengers and swelling the ranks of other well-known Super Hero teams!

Being over 100 years old, professional soldier Logan has fought in the world's bloodiest wars—assuming that what he remembers of his youth is true!

Wolverine can regenerate from any injury, short of losing his head. The speed of his healing depends on the nature and extent of his wounds.

It's never wise to pick a fight with Wolverine.

Weapon X

Wolverine was born James Howlett in Alberta, Canada, in the late 19th century. The son of wealthy landowners, he did not enjoy a happy childhood. Often frail and sickly, James was virtually house-bound until, after the murder of his father, his three bone claws first appeared and he was forced to flee his home. The youth took to a life of wandering where hard labor and being out in all weathers toughened his body and triggered a latent mutant healing factor. James began to use the retractable bone claws on his hands as weapons, enhancing his natural ferocity. Able to regenerate from almost any injury, James aged far more slowly than those around him, traveling the world for nearly a century as "Logan" (named after one of his few childhood friends). Ever the loner, Logan has been a samurai, soldier, and spy, unsheathing his claws in berserker rages when backed into a corner. Decades ago, Logan volunteered for the Canadian military's "Weapon X" program, where he underwent terrible physical and mental suffering during a horrific process to lace his bones and claws with Adamantium, a nigh-indestructible metal. In the years that followed, Logan struggled to regain lost memories and sort out his true origins from the many false memories implanted during the agonizing Weapon X experiments. Codenamed "Wolverine," he eventually joined the X-Men, a team of mutants seeking to make the world a better place for both mankind and mutants. After the Super Villain prison break from the Raft, Captain America asked Wolverine to fight alongside the Avengers as well.

Logan joined Professor Charles Xavier's X-Men, where he became a loyal and trusted member of the mutant team, often serving as field commander.

Sheathed in Adamantium, Wolverine's claws can cut through any substance like a hot knife through butter! His Adamantium laced bones, too, are virtually unbreakable.

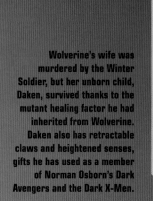

Wolverine's wife was murdered by the Winter Soldier, but her unborn child, Daken, survived thanks to the mutant healing factor he had inherited from Wolverine. Daken also has retractable claws and heightened senses, gifts he has used as a member of Norman Osborn's Dark Avengers and the Dark X-Men.

Heightened strength makes Wolverine able to bear easily the 300 pounds of weight his Adamantium skeleton adds to his frame.

Years of traveling have made Logan fluent in Japanese, Russian, Chinese, and several Native American dialects.

Wolverine has mastered nearly every fighting style he has encountered on his wanderings.

"HEY, I'M AN X-MAN AND ON TWO AVENGERS TEAMS... MULTITASKING. IT'S MY MUTANT POWER. DON'T TELL ANYBODY."

In addition to serving both Earth's Mightiest Heroes and the X-Men, Wolverine has been a member of the Fantastic Four, Secret Defenders, Alpha Flight, X-Force, Team Weapon X, and various other military brigades.

WARRIOR'S CODE
Logan has long had an affinity for Japan. He has studied the samurai way and mastered many of its martial arts, including the use of the deadly katana. In Japan, Logan met his late wife Itsu and later romanced the doomed Mariko Yashida, something that brought him into conflict with the Yakuza's Clan Yashida and the Silver Samurai.

KEY DATA

REAL NAME James Howlett (Logan)

OCCUPATION Adventurer, former spy

AFFILIATIONS Current: X-Men, the Avengers

POWERS/WEAPONS Mutant healing factor; Adamantium-laced skeleton and retractable claws (three extending from the backs of each wrist); superhuman senses, strength, and endurance.

ECHO

Maya Lopez had a less-than-conservative upbringing, having been raised by Kingpin Wilson Fisk after Fisk murdered her father and blamed Daredevil for the crime. Ironically, Daredevil's alter-ego, Matt Murdock, was later Maya's lover. Though deaf, Maya possesses unique memory skills, making her able to perfectly recall and mimic any physical action she sees. Thus, she is a martial arts and acrobatic savant, having first served as an Avenger in the guise of Ronin. Presently, she refers to herself as Echo since her abilities allow her to imitate and match the fighting

2000s New

For the new millennium, Earth's Mightiest Super Heroes added two martial arts savants, a super-being with a questionable hold on sanity, another thundering god, one more super-genius, a mysterious replacement for Captain America, and a sorcerer supreme to its swelling ranks!

PRINCE OF POWER

Super-genius Amadeus Cho can perform amazing mental calculations in seconds, making him "the smartest guy in the room" at Avengers HQ… assuming Hank Pym isn't around, that is. The former "Mastermind Excello" was given the title Prince of Power following the death of his friend Hercules. As such, Cho now wields Hercules's adamantine mace in addition to the wealth and resources of the so-called Olympus Group. Cho also uses the helmet of late Ant-Man Scott Lang to grant himself formidable telepathic abilities. Cho's constant companion is Kerberos the coyote, "Kirby" for short.

THE SENTRY

A secret serum gave Robert Reynolds miraculous psionic powers, as well as superstrength, superspeed, the ability to fly, and invulnerability. Unfortunately, the serum also unleashed the darker side of Reynolds' psyche, in the form of the Void, Sentry's worst enemy. Sentry defeated the Void by mind-wiping the world's populace, making each and every person—including himself— forget that Sentry ever existed. With no Sentry, there was no Void. Returning decades later, Sentry has reclaimed his life and serves as an Avenger in good standing after casting the also-returned Void into the heart of the sun.

ARES

Olympian God of War Ares was a frequent foe of the Avengers on Earth. But following the Superhuman Registration Act, Ares accepted an invitation to join the Avengers as a salaried Super Hero. The living manifestation of warfare, Ares can wield any weapon from any era with deadly skill. He is immortal and superhuman in every physical way, and can only be harmed by magical means.

CAPTAIN AMERICA

Once Cap's sidekick, Buchanan "Bucky" Barnes was believed to have perished in the same accident that resulted in Cap's long suspended animation. But Bucky's still living body was retrieved by agents of the Soviet Union, who used memory implantation techniques to make an amnesiac Barnes into an assassin known as the Winter Soldier. Immersed in hibernation-like stasis between missions, Barnes' memories were eventually restored. Later, when Cap was believed assassinated, Barnes was recruited to the Avengers by Iron Man and secretly given autonomy, though this was illegal, following the Registration Act.

IRON FIST

Iron Fist Wields a punch that packs a metal-hard wallop. As a boy, Danny Rand visited the fabled city of K'un-Lun, where a decade of martial arts training forged him into a fighting champion. Able to focus his natural energy (chi) into his hands, Iron Fist can heal the injuries of himself and others. Previously a "hero-for-hire" alongside friend and partner Luke Cage (Power Man), Iron Fist has joined Cage as a full-time Avenger.

DR. STRANGE

Former sorcerer, Dr. Stephen Strange lost some of his mystical might after wielding dark magic to stop a rampaging Hulk. Previously, Strange's arcane arsenal included the Eye of Agamotto and the Cloak of Levitation, as well as a vast library of books on magic. For a time, Strange hosted the New Avengers and allowed his home to be used as the team's base. An Avenger still, Strange is exploring the limits of his downgraded but still quite formidable powers.

THE YOUNG AVENGERS

NEW BLOOD

The Young Avengers' current lineup includes Wiccan, Stature, Hulkling, Hawkeye II, and Patriot. This new generation of Earth's Mightiest Heroes is based in the abandoned Bishop Publishing building.

ORIGINS

When the time-traveling tyrant Kang the Conqueror visited his 31st-century teenage self, Nathaniel Richards, the shocked teen was horrified to see what he would become a thousand years hence. Wearing a suit of neuro-kinetic armor—a gift from Kang—Richards traveled back in time, hoping to find the Avengers and enlist them to help him change the future. He found that the Avengers had disbanded. The armor would not allow him to go any further back in time, so Richards gathered a group of superpowered youths and created his own team of heroes, who were dubbed "Young Avengers" by the press. Richards became Iron Lad, and led fellow teen heroes Hulkling, Asgardian, and Patriot to thwart Kang's plans, which included defeating the so-called Growing Man, a robot sent back in time to fetch Richards and prevent any paradoxes from interrupting Kang's diabolical destiny! Though formed to thwart Kang, the Young Avengers had many notable exploits during the Skrull Invasion and continue to be a force for good in any era.

IRON LAD

Nathaniel Richards is determined not to become Kang the Conqueror. As Iron Lad, he possesses the secret of time travel and wears psychokinetic armor that obeys his every thought, allowing him to fly, fire energy blasts, and project force fields.

HULKLING

Theodore "Teddy" Altman is Dorrek VIII, the shape-changing son of Captain Marvel and a Skrull princess. When the Skrulls invaded Earth, the Super-Skrull sent to bring Teddy back to the Skrull Empire left Teddy on Earth and himself returned as Hulkling!

PATRIOT

Elijah Bradley is the grandson of Isaiah Bradley, the African-American Captain America active during World War II. Elijah used MGH (Mutant Growth Hormone) to replicate Isaiah's powers until a blood transfusion from Isaiah gave him real superpowers.

THE VISION

Destroyed by the Scarlet Witch, the Vision was rebuilt by Iron Lad who added operating systems from his own armor. As well as density-controlling powers and energy-beam emissions, the Vision holds invaluable files on the next generation of potential heroes.

WICCAN

William "Billy" Kaplan was once called Asgardian, but renamed himself Wiccan because of his ability to alter reality, cast spells, and levitate. These hex-like abilities make Billy believe he is the son of the Scarlet Witch.

HAWKEYE

Wealthy Katherine "Kate" Elizabeth Bishop began martial arts and weapons training after being attacked in New York's Central Park. Later, she joined the Young Avengers and took up the bow and name of Hawkeye when the longtime Avenger was presumed dead.

SPEED

Like Wiccan, Thomas "Tommy" Shepherd is thought to be a lost child of the Scarlet Witch. As Speed, he is faster than the speed of sound and can create ultra-velocity vibrations that disrupt the atomic structure of objects, with explosive results!

STATURE

Like her father Scott Lang (Ant-Man), Cassandra "Cassie" Eleanor Lang gained size-changing abilities via Pym Particles. Her powers are linked to her emotions; embarrassment makes her a literal shrinking violet. She is romantically linked to the Vision.

RUNAWAYS

The Runaways are a group of teens whose superpowered parents belonged to a secret cabal called the Pride. The Pride engaged in ritual sacrifice to appease their gods, the Gibborim, and to ensure that six of their number would rule over an Earthly paradise. After rejecting their families, the children ran away and used their inherited powers to end the Pride's dominance over Los Angeles. Unfortunately, the city has since become infested with Super Villains, a problem the Runaways have taken on themselves. They have worked with the Young Avengers on a few occasions.

BRUISER

Mutant Molly Hayes is the youngest Runaway and one of only 198 mutants to retain her powers following the Scarlet Witch's restructuring of reality.

SISTER GRIMM

Nico Minoru wields the Staff of One, which allows her to cast any spell—but only once. She can only summon the Staff of One when her own blood is drawn.

TALKBACK

When smart-talking Chase Stein ran away, he took weapons created by his mad-scientist parents, including "Fistigon" gauntlets and multi-spectral goggles.

LUCY IN THE SKY

Born of extraterrestrials, Karolina Dean can fly, project energy blasts, and create force fields. Her blood is deadly to vampires. When the sun goes down, her powers wane.

VICTOR MANCHA

Victor is an intelligent cyborg made of parts from a duplicate Ultron and donor DNA from a petty criminal. He has control over electromagnetic energy.

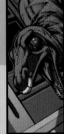

ARSENIC AND OLD LACE

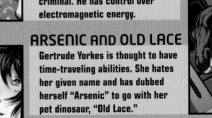

Gertrude Yorkes is thought to have time-traveling abilities. She hates her given name and has dubbed herself "Arsenic" to go with her pet dinosaur, "Old Lace."

KLARA PRAST

Also known as "Tower of Flower" and "Rose Red," Klara has the ability to "talk" to plants, manipulating the growth of any flora as she pleases.

CIVIL WAR

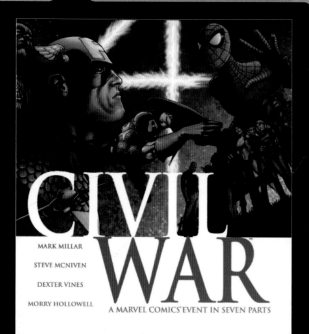

MARK MILLAR
STEVE MCNIVEN
DEXTER VINES
MORRY HOLLOWELL

A MARVEL COMICS EVENT IN SEVEN PARTS

1

Publication Date
July 2006

Editor in Chief
Joe Quesada

Cover Artist
Steve McNiven

Writer
Mark Millar

Penciler
Steve McNiven

Inker
Dexter Vines

Colorist
Morry Hollowell

#1

"Cap going underground means every Super Hero who disagrees with us suddenly has a figurehead."
The U.S. President

Main Characters: Captain America; Iron Man; Maria Hill

Main Supporting Characters: New Warriors; Nitro, Spider-Woman; Goliath; Ms. Marvel; Wolverine; the Fantastic Four; Dr. Strange; the Watcher

Main Locations: Stamford; New York; the Baxter Building; SHIELD Helicarrier; Washington D.C.

BACKGROUND

Company-wide crossovers were nothing new to the comic book community in 2006, but Marvel Comics' *Civil War* was a game-changer for the entire Marvel Universe. This time, Marvel's heroes and heroines didn't face the usual Earth-shattering cosmic threat or alien invasion. With an ad campaign that challenged readers to decide "Whose side are you on?" *Civil War* began with an explosive catastrophe that would ultimately force the Avengers and virtually every other costumed champion to face a government-mandated Superhuman Registration Act. With its heroic community split down the middle, Marvel began the chronicle of a radical new age of sanctioned superhumans… and the outlaw vigilantes who refused to compromise their identities and the safety of their loved ones!

The Story

In the history of Super Heroes versus Super Villains, there has always been the tacit threat of collateral damage to innocent bystanders and property. Before the Civil War, the human population accepted this risk in the battle for the greater good. That all changed when the neophyte New Warriors picked a fight with four superior villains in Stamford, Connecticut...

"Stars" of a low-rated reality television show, **(1)** the wannabe Super Heroes known as the New Warriors (Speedball, Night Thrasher, Namorita, and Microbe) tracked four on-the-run Super Villains (Speedfreek, Coldheart, Cobalt Man, and Nitro) to Stamford. Spoiling for a fight and celebrity status, the New Warriors started a super-melee that ended explosively when Nitro killed the fledgling heroes and more than 900 civilians in a fireball that decimated Stamford **(2)**.

As public opinion shifted away from its costumed champions, Tony Stark (a.k.a. Iron Man) felt the emotional impact of a grieving mother whose child perished in the catastrophe **(3)**. Later, things got even uglier as a crowd waiting in line at a Manhattan hotspot turned against Johnny Storm (a.k.a. the Human Torch). The unruly mob beat a blindsided Johnny senseless as Americans lost trust in their self-appointed Super Hero defenders **(4)**.

Subsequently, the President of the United States began legislation of the Superhuman Registration Act, which prompted an assembly spanning Avengers and other prominent heroes and heroines gathered at the Fantastic Four's Baxter Building headquarters to debate the pros and cons of revealing their identities and working as paid protectors of the U.S. government **(5)**.

Meanwhile, Captain America—a vocal opponent of the Superhuman Registration Act—fought for his principles aboard the airborne SHIELD Helicarrier against agents prepared to arrest any hero who didn't voluntarily comply **(6)**.

As the heroes below decided just where they stood on the controversial law, Spider-Woman commented on the appearance of the Watcher in their midst **(7)**, a portent of momentous events to follow: a civil war between heroes loyal to Captain America and the newly sanctioned superhumans led by Iron Man **(8)**!

> "His name is the Watcher, Spider-Woman, and he only appears to record moments of great change and enormous upheaval. His presence now does not bode well."
>
> Dr. Strange

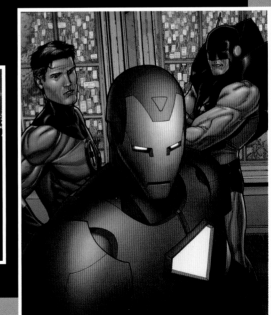

CIVIL WAR

The appearance in the sky of the Watcher, recorder of momentous events, did not bode well. The events that followed would be momentous indeed, splitting the Super Hero community asunder in a civil war that turned Avenger against Avenger, patriot against patriot, friend against friend.

TAKING SIDES

The Stamford Incident (see pages 150–151) was the final straw. Government regulation of costumed heroes had long been mooted. Now influential pressmen like *The Daily Bugle*'s J. Jonah Jameson demanded immediate action: "No more masks and no more excuses about creepy secret identities. These clowns finally work for SHIELD or they throw their butts in jail." Responding to public outcry, Congress passed the Superhuman Registration Act (SRA). All superpowered individuals had to register their real names, thus revealing secret identities. They also needed legal authorization to fight crime. Iron Man and Mr. Fantastic (Reed Richards) were determined to enforce the Act. However, Captain America adamantly opposed it, believing that Super Heroes could become tools of a repressive state. Cap clashed violently with Iron Man and SHIELD officers and went into hiding. He thus became a focal point for opposition to the Act. A Super Hero civil war had broken out.

Spider-Man Peter Parker was worried about jeopardizing his secret identity, but Tony Stark managed to persuade him to abide by the Act. Stark was at Peter's side at the ensuing press announcement.

The ideological clash between Iron Man and Cap—government control versus the rights of the individual—descended into brutal violence.

THE DEATH OF GOLIATH

Captain America formed the Secret Avengers, comprising himself, Hercules, Goliath, Iron Fist (posing as Daredevil), Falcon, and Cable. They were later joined by other heroes, including Cloak and Dagger. The Secret Avengers were lured into a trap by Iron Man's Pro-Reg force. Cap and Iron Man tried to resolve their differences, but talks broke down and a Thor clone devised by Reed Richards and Hank Pym ran amok and killed Goliath, exacerbating the conflict. Invisible Woman (Susan Richards) was so angered by her husband Reed's involvement that she split from him.

WHOSE

The killing of Goliath and the creation of 42, a Negative Zone prison for heroes, led Spider-Man to have grave doubts about Iron Man's stance and tactics. After a violent clash, Spider-Man went "rogue."

THUNDERBOLTS

As the conflict escalated, SHIELD took the risky step of enlisting the Thunderbolts team of super-criminals (below) to capture anti-Reg heroes. Electric implants were supposed to control them, but their methods were brutal. Ordered to use minimum force, The Jester and Jack O'Lantern took great delight in "kicking the crap" out of Spider-Man when Spidey went on the run.

Spider-Man was rescued by the Punisher, who took him to Captain America's secret HQ for medical attention. Incensed that SHIELD was now employing thieves and killers, the Punisher joined Cap's Secret Avengers.

CAP SURRENDERS

42, the Negative Zone jail at Ryker's Island prison set up by Tony Stark and Reed Richards to hold superpowered individuals, was always a likely target for Captain America rebels. The two opposing forces met outside and a fearsome battle ensued. Just as Cap's forces seemed to be gaining the upper hand, Captain America himself, disillusioned by the continuing violence, decided to surrender and told his troops to "stand down."

Iron Man's pro-Registration forces faced Captain America's Secret Avengers in a showdown outside the 42 jail for heroes.

Cap realized that he had lost the Registration argument when he was attacked by a mob of ordinary civilians. The devastation the civil war was causing horrified him.

THE 50-STATE INITIATIVE

With the end of the civil war, a grateful president made Tony Stark director of SHIELD. He announced the launch of the 50-State Initiative—an authorized Super Hero team in every U.S. state, not only fighting crime but also improving social conditions.

SIDE ARE YOU ON?

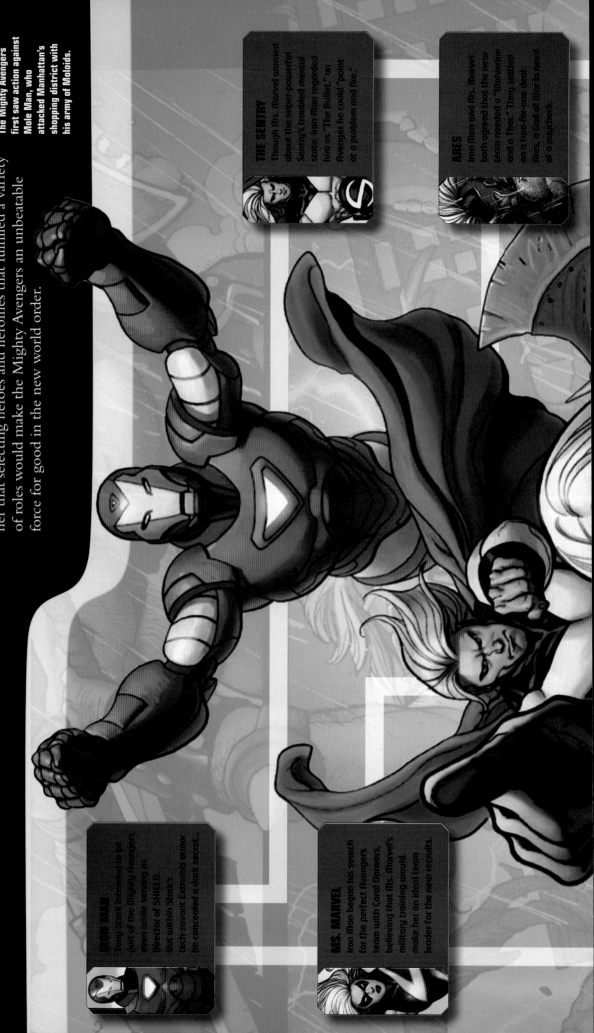

THE MIGHTY AVENGERS

ORIGINS

After the civil war, Iron Man's Avengers Initiative offered a new start for Earth's Mightiest Heroes under the aegis of the reformed SHIELD, now commanded by Tony Stark. Iron Man chose Carol Danvers (Ms. Marvel) to lead a new Avengers team and together they sorted through every hero and heroine filed under the Superhuman Registration Act to pick the new roster. Ms. Marvel suggested an all-star team of powerhouse protectors, but Iron Man convinced her that selecting heroes and heroines that fulfilled a variety of roles would make the Mighty Avengers an unbeatable force for good in the new world order.

The Mighty Avengers first saw action against Mole Man, who attacked Manhattan's shopping district with his army of Moloids.

THE SENTRY
Though Ms. Marvel worried about the super-powerful Sentry's troubled mental state, Iron Man regarded him as "The Bullet," an Avenger he could "point at a problem and fire."

ARES
Iron Man and Ms. Marvel both agreed that the new team needed a "Wolverine and a Thor." They settled on Ares, a God of War in need of a paycheck.

IRON MAN
Tony Stark intended to be part of the Mighty Avengers even while serving as Director of SHIELD. But within Stark's tech-savant Extremis armor he concealed a dark secret.

MS. MARVEL
Iron Man began his search for the perfect Avengers team with Carol Danvers, believing that Ms. Marvel's military training would make her an ideal team leader for the new recruits.

After trouncing Mole Man, the new team faced a trial by fire when Iron Man's armor liquefied before their eyes, transforming him into a lithe female form—the latest version of Ultron! Reconstituted from Iron Man's Extremis armor and resembling the Wasp, the Avengers' android foe intended to rain nuclear fire upon mankind.

155

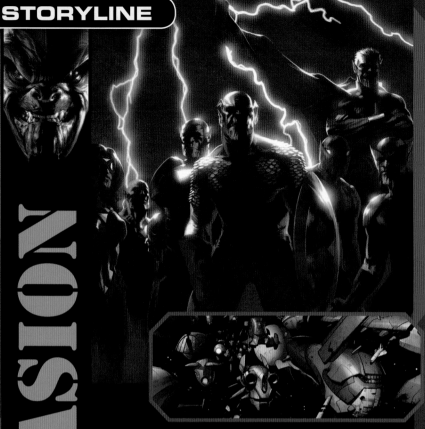

SECRET INVASION

When a malevolent alien species, the Skrulls, secretly invaded Earth, nobody was safe. The villains could take over the bodies and minds of anyone they chose—without being noticed! Who could be trusted?

SAVAGE TIMES

A Skrull ship had crash-landed in the Savage Land, a "lost world" in the Antarctic and the Avengers went to investigate. Iron Man's suit (along with Stark Enterprises' weapons facilities back home) was attacked by a Skrull computer virus. Then a squad of familiar-looking heroes poured from the Skrull ship. These heroes claimed that they had been captured by Skrulls and escaped. Utter confusion reigned in the Avengers' ranks until Reed Richards showed up with his newly invented Skrull detector beam and sorted out the real heroes from the Skrull imposters.

ALIEN DISCOVERY

Iron Man's discovery that Elektra, leader of the ninja assassin group the Hand was, in reality, a Skrull—the first major indication that a Skrull invasion of Earth had begun. Just as Reed Richards was about to discover the secret of the Skrulls' shapeshifting powers, he was disabled by a Skrull posing as Yellowjacket Hank Pym and taken aboard a Skrull ship. Skrull technicians were eager to study their most formidable foe.

Reed Richards, the Fantastic Four's Mr. Fantastic, never suspected that his associate Hank Pym was a shapeshifting Skrull.

Keeping scientific genius Reed Richards a prisoner was vital to the Skrulls. Fortunately for the human race, Reed was rescued by SWORD agent Abigail Brand.

TARGET: NEW YORK

While more Skrulls were dispatched to join the battle in the Savage Land, others attacked all over the world... including the Blue Area of the Moon, home of the Inhumans! A new breed of Super-Skrulls with powers stolen from Earth's heroes laid siege to Times Square as New York City became a target for the invasion!

The Secret Invasion was part of a larger plan to conquer Earth and convince the surviving population that Skrull dominion would improve human culture.

When Skrull forces met with mild protest, the regime revealed its brutal nature. But vital help—Reed Richards and the Avengers—was on its way from the Savage Land.

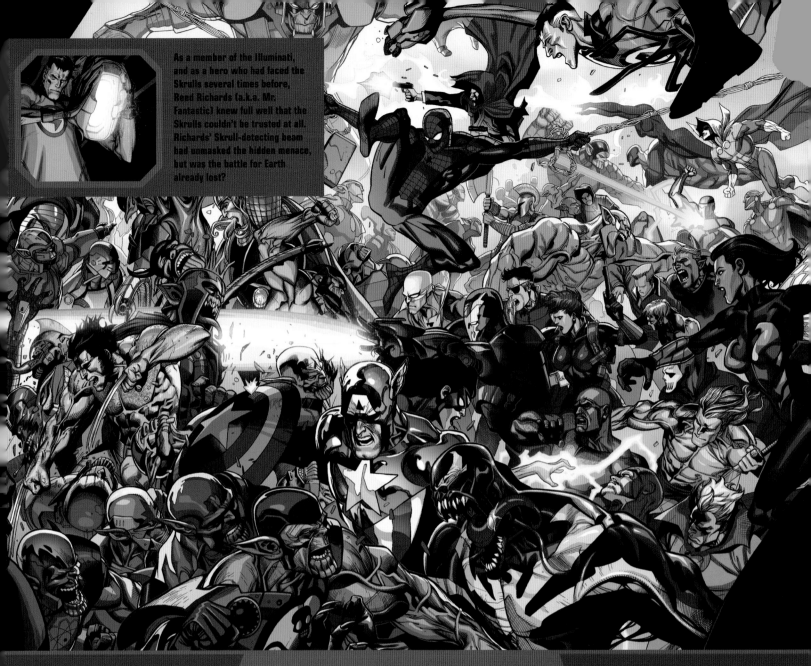

As a member of the Illuminati, and as a hero who had faced the Skrulls several times before, Reed Richards (a.k.a. Mr. Fantastic) knew full well that the Skrulls couldn't be trusted at all. Richards' Skrull-detecting beam had unmasked the hidden menace, but was the battle for Earth already lost?

THE FINAL CONFLICT

Even Tony Stark was fooled by the near-perfection of a Skrull disguise when his faithful butler Jarvis was discovered to be an alien mole, sabotaging the Avengers' computer systems with a techno-virus that soon spread to all Stark technology across the globe. The SHIELD Helicarrier dropped like a stone from the sky, while Iron Man's Extremis armor shut down. Nick Fury came out of hiding to lead his Secret Warriors to rescue the Young Avengers, but the tide of battle had turned against them. When all seemed lost, the Skrull Queen Veranke, visited Tony Stark disguised as Spider-Woman and attempted to convince the defeated Iron Man that he was, in fact, also a Skrull.

Stark donned new, uncompromised armor for a final battle as Earth's Mightiest Heroes amassed to fight the Skrulls to the death. But in the end, it was the scheming Norman Osborn who thwarted the Skrull invasion when he killed Veranke in a coup de grace broadcast around the world. The Secret Invasion was over, but not without massive casualties amongst Earth's Mightiest Heroes. To many, the Avengers had failed to save the world this time.

Queen Veranke's plan was enacted when the Wasp activated her altered growth serum. As destructive energies built up within the Wasp's expanding body, her teammate Thor had no choice but to destroy her to save innumerable lives.

In the invasion's aftermath, SHIELD was shut down and Norman Osborn—now viewed as Earth's greatest hero—began to restructure the remnants of SHIELD into HAMMER. Osborn began assembling his own Dark Avengers. It would seem that the Skrulls weren't the only villains hiding in plain sight...

DARK REIGN

When Norman Osborn succeeded Tony Stark as government liaison for superhuman affairs, he invited fellow Super Villains to form a sinister cabal. The Dark Reign had begun...

The Cabal consisted of Emma Frost, Dr. Doom, Norman Osborn, Loki, Sub-Mariner, and the Hood. Taskmaster joined later.

Morgan Le Fay came close to destroying Osborn's Avengers on the team's first ever mission.

HAMMER TIME

As Norman Osborn took control of HAMMER, he used his new position to settle old scores and increase his own powerbase. Tony Stark destroyed all copies of the Superhuman Registration Act to protect the identities of his fellow heroes from Osborn. The only remaining source for the information was Stark's own brain, forcing Stark to go on the run and try to wipe the it from his own mind. Osborn infiltrated one of Stark's labs and found a collection of old Iron Man armor. He used the tech to create a new heroic identity for himself—the Iron Patriot. Osborn used his new alter ego to lead his own team of Avengers. He recruited Thunderbolt members Moonstone, Venom, and Bullseye to the new team, giving them the identities of Ms. Marvel, Spider-Man, and Hawkeye. He also brought in Wolverine's estranged son, Daken (as Wolverine), Ares, the mentally unstable Sentry, and Noh-Varr (as Captain Marvel). The team's first mission—to save Dr. Doom from attack by a vengeful Morgan Le Fay—was nearly their last, as the witch kept returning from the past each time she was stopped. Osborn and Doom eventually went back in time to kill Morgan before she could ever attack them.

Osborn's X-Men team included: the Mimic, Daken (as Wolverine), Prince Namor, Emma Frost, Weapon Omega, Cloak, and Dagger.

DARK X-MEN

Osborn also tried to take control of the X-Men's legacy by creating his own team of government-backed X-Men. The team consisted of Daken (again in his Wolverine identity), Mimic, Weapon Omega (Michael Pointer, whose powers stemmed from the energy dispersed when mutants lost their powers following House of M), Prince Namor, and Emma Frost. Mystique was hired to mimic Professor X but wasn't active in the field while the Dark Beast (an evil version of Hank McCoy) was employed to experiment on captured mutants. The team had an uneasy alliance with the New Avengers and fell apart when they were pitted against the real X-Men. Emma Frost and Namor had been working for the X-Men's leader, Scott Summers (Cyclops), all along and turned against Osborn's teams. When Osborn's Avengers and remaining Dark X-Men were sent to stop Scott's X-Men, they were defeated live on TV. Osborn tried to turn it into a victory through the media but it signified the start of his fall from power.

UNREAL WORLD

By the time the Dark Avengers were sent to Dinosaur, Colorado, in search of a missing politician's daughter, the pressure was starting to affect Osborn and his Green Goblin persona was threatening to return. Events in Dinosaur only made his mental state worse. The Molecule Man had reshaped reality in the town and used his powers to move a few atoms around in Osborn's brain. While the Sentry eventually destroyed Molecule Man, the fight left the Sentry more powerful and unstable than ever.

The Molecule Man had created a hellish home for himself in the town of Dinosaur, Colorado.

THE END BEGINS...

As his Avengers returned to base, Osborn started to struggle internally as his Green Goblin insanity became more dominant. His fragile mental state made it all the easier for Loki to convince him to launch an all-out assault on Asgard. An act that would bring about the end of Osborn's dark reign...

SIEGE

The dark reign of Norman Osborn was the low point for many of the world's heroes. When Loki convinced Osborn to attack Asgard it signified the start of one of the most brutal fights in Avengers' history and Osborn's fall from power.

When the valiant Volstagg left Asgard seeking adventure, he sought to help mortals—as his friend Thor had done.

A CALL TO ARMS

Norman Osborn was in charge of HAMMER and in a position of power. It was a situation that was never going to end well. His reign as government liaison came to a close in dramatic fashion when Loki convinced him to attack Asgard. The two villains manipulated events to set Volstagg up as the fall guy, initiating a fight between the Asgardian and the villainous U-Foes that resulted in a massive explosion at a Chicago sport's stadium. Ignoring a Presidential order to stand down, Osborn declared war on Asgard. He led his Dark Avengers team and the military forces of HAMMER into the attack.

When Osborn and Loki used the U-Foes to attack Volstagg, the ensuing battle caused an explosion that destroyed Soldier Field in Chicago, a stadium filled with fans watching a football game.

Loki was playing his own game and warned Balder of the impending attack. The two powerful forces clashed, with Thor taking the fight to Osborn's Avengers only to be knocked unconscious as the team used all their firepower against him. Thor was saved by Maria Hill and soon returned to the fray. Steve Rogers, recently reborn after being lost in time, watched events with horror and, donning the Captain America uniform for the first time since his return, summoned all the other Avengers to his side to help the Asgardians. To combat the heroes, Osborn called on crime boss the Hood's Super Villains to fight on his side. The two vast armies clashed on the fields surrounding Asgard. Tony Stark was already in the nearby town of Broxton recovering from a life-saving procedure to restore his mind. Despite his frail state, he left his sick bed to fight as Iron Man and reclaim his stolen armor from an increasingly insane Norman Osborn.

Norman Osborn, as the Iron Patriot, led the combined forces of the Dark Avengers and HAMMER into battle against Asgard and the Norse Gods.

GOD OF WAR

At first, Ares refused to take up arms against the Asgardians until Osborn convinced him that Loki had taken over the realm. When Ares learned this was a lie, he turned on his erstwhile allies and came close to killing Osborn. The Sentry intervened and not only killed Ares but tore the god apart.

Osborn's forces seemed to be gaining the upper hand against the Asgardians until Captain America arrived with a host of Avengers. The first Osborn knew of the attack was when Cap's shield knocked him off his feet. It signified the beginning of the end for Osborn's dark reign.

When Norman Osborn was defeated and his Iron Patriot armor removed, the heroes were shocked to see his face painted green as his insane alter-ego rose to the fore once again. He declared that he was the only one able to control the Sentry and stop the Void returning.

THE VOID

The transformation of the Sentry into the Void gave the heroes their biggest threat yet. In the end, Loki sacrificed his own life to try and weaken the Void—although even when Iron Man sent HAMMER's Helicarrier crashing into the Void, it failed to kill him. As a weakened Sentry started to become the Void once more, Thor was forced to kill him.

ASGARD DESTROYED

As the fight started to turn against Osborn's forces, the villain issued one last order—for the Sentry to destroy Asgard. The Sentry crashed through Asgard's foundations, bringing the Realm Eternal crashing down to Earth. In the ruins, a horrified Loki saw that his plans were coming to nothing and decided to make amends. Begging his father for help, Loki used sorcery to empower the heroes and then launched himself at the Sentry, who was now fully transformed into the Void.

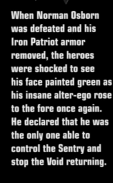

As the Void started to take control again, Thor was forced to kill him before flying to the sun to bury his friend.

AFTERMATH

Once the dust had settled, HAMMER was shut down and Steve Rogers replaced Norman Osborn as the new executive in charge of America's Super Heroes. Thor and his fellow Asgardians told Rogers that they owed the humans a huge debt and Thor would fight alongside the Avengers whenever he was needed. For his part, Rogers was already making plans for the new world order. One that would signal the beginning of the age of the hero.

ALTERNATIVE AVENGERS

It should come as no shock that Super Heroes rarely populate just one universe. The Marvel pantheon isn't just limited to a single planet, but countless parallel worlds in a dizzying daisy-chain that add up to a Multiverse of multiple Earths, multiple Avengers, and multiple histories for all the Avengers. In the Ultimate universe, Captain America is thawed from his decades-long hibernation in time to join an Avengers team bracing for alien domination. On a post-apocalyptic Earth, every last hero is a flesh-eating Marvel Zombie! And even on worlds recognizable to most, divergent timelines emerge to create new pasts, presents, and futures! Through every permutation of these alternative Avengers, one constant remains: heroism endures through time and space, and Earth(s)'s Mightiest Heroes will fight to the end of one world only to be reborn in the next...

1950s

The present-day Avengers aren't the first costumed champions to call themselves "Avengers." As early as 1950, a team of superpowered individuals used that appellation when they joined forces to save the President of the United States!

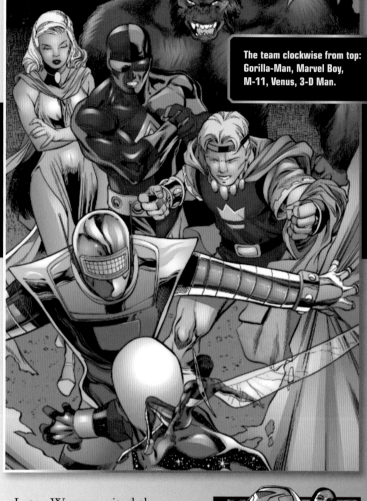

The team clockwise from top: Gorilla-Man, Marvel Boy, M-11, Venus, 3-D Man.

CHINESE THREAT

In 1958, this team of heroes was known as Department Zero. G-Man Jimmy Woo recruited his former "Avengers" associates to save President Eisenhower from Yellow Claw, a Chinese criminal mastermind bent on world domination. Department Zero included Namora, Marvel Boy (later the Uranian), Venus, Gorilla-Man, and M-11 (formerly the Human Robot) as part of the team who rescued Eisenhower from Yellow Claw's organization. The team was disbanded by the government after nearly a year.

Later, Woo reunited the team to investigate the Atlas Foundation, a front for Yellow Claw's criminal empire. Yellow Claw was actually Plan Chu, a descendant of Ghengis Khan, who used the Foundation and his conflict with Jimmy Woo to mold Woo into his successor. Jimmy eventually accepted this role and turned the Atlas Foundation into a force for good.

The criminal Jade Claw once had a relationship with Jimmy Woo.

Agents of...

In order to undermine Norman Osborn's Initiative, the Atlas Foundation brokered an arms deal that brought the Agents into conflict with the new Avengers team, who wanted to destroy the weapons rather than let them to fall into Osborn's hands. However, Spider-Man's spider-sense told him that the Agents of Atlas weren't the enemies that the Avengers believed them to be.

1959 Black Ops

While hunting down ex-Nazi war criminals in the late 1950s, Nick Fury was tasked by the President to assemble an Avengers Black Ops group for a secret mission involving none other than the Red Skull! Fury's team included former Howling Commando Dum Dum Dugan, Victor Creed (Sabertooth), the Atlantean Princess Namora, Russian operative Ernst Sablinova (the Silver Sable), monster hunter Ulysses Bloodstone, Sergei Kravinoff (Kraven the Hunter), and dashing soldier-for-hire Dominic Fortune! The team tracked the Red Skull to Sweden, determined to stop their Nazi nemesis and recover the mysterious contents of the Red Skull's briefcase!

"Why did the Nazis make themselves a Captain America?"

Namora

Dominic Fortune

Dum Dum Dugan

Sabertooth

Ulysses Bloodstone

Kraven the Hunter

Red Skull Rising

The Red Skull was a successor to the original. He had created a Nazi Captain America using a variant of the Super Soldier Serum and Infinity Formula (which Fury used to stay young). Decades later, this formula was used to save Mockingbird's life.

A-NEXT

THUNDERSTRIKE   **MAINFRAME**   **J2**   **STINGER**   **JARVIS**

Throughout the Multiverse, there are many Earths, each with a parallel reality or alternate future. In one possible reality, the Avengers had disbanded and their mansion had become a museum overseen by Jarvis. History often repeats itself, however, and Loki manipulated events, leading to the formation of a new team of Avengers.

TROLLS ATTACK!

Just after Kevin Masterson, son of the deceased Avenger Thunderstrike, visited Jarvis and learned that his father's enchanted mace still existed, Avengers Mansion was attacked by Asgardian trolls! Jarvis sent out the signal for the Avengers to assemble and was surprised at the costumed adventurers who responded, including Cassandra Lang (Stinger, daughter of the former Ant-Man Scott Lang), Zane Yama (J2, son of the unstoppable Juggernaut), Jubilation Lee (Jubilee, now leader of the X-People), and Mainframe, an upgraded Iron Man program modeled on the encephalograms of Tony Stark. Together with Kevin Masterson, these "next generation" heroes fought back. But they were taken prisoner and transported to Asgard.

Among the heroes who first arrived to battle the trolls were Mainframe, Jolt, and J2, all "second-generation" Super Heroes.

THE LOKI CONNECTION

As with the very first team of Avengers, the "A-Next" roster assembled in response to a threat from Loki, the Asgardian God of Lies, who dispatched the trolls to steal the enchanted mace of Eric Masterson (Thunderstrike). Thunderstrike's mace was forged on Asgard by the command of Odin—Loki's father and ruler of the Norse gods—and possessed unimaginable power!

SIBLING RIVALRY

Loki's evil plan was to set Asgard aflame and tear the heavens asunder! But to do so, the God of Lies needed to unleash the magic stored within Thunderstrike's mace. By combining the mace's power with his own sorcery, Loki would finally be powerful enough to defeat his hated half-brother Thor, whose mighty uru hammer, Mjolnir, was also forged on Asgard.

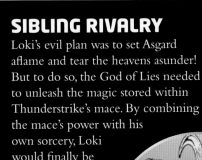

Within his hidden base on the Isle of Silence, the God of Lies rallied his monstrous army.

Before Loki could claim the mace, Kevin Masterson seized it and absorbed all its might into his body!

ASSEMBLED AGAIN

Now possessing the full powers of Thunderstrike, Kevin Masterson led the young heroes against Loki's forces. Of course, the cowardly Loki fled when all seemed lost, and the remaining trolls

As Jarvis watched, a lump stuck in his throat, four of Earth's soon-to-be Mightiest Heroes made history... AGAIN.

and other Asgardian menaces retreated when Thor made his presence known in a crash of lightning. Upon their return home, the heroes agreed that Earth still needed a team of protectors and decided to assemble an all-new Avengers. While Jolt, Speedball, and Jubilee opted to serve as reservists, Thunderstrike Mainframe, Stinger, and J2 formed the core team of Earth's Next Mightiest Heroes, soon to be joined by many other recruits.

This team of alternate Avengers included (clockwise from top): J2, Jubilee, Thunderstrike, Mainframe, Speedball, and Stinger.

"Which one of you guys sent out that Avengers distress call?"
Jubilee

THE ULTIMATES

In a different reality and universe altogether, on Earth-1610, there exists a group of avenging costumed adventurers called the Ultimates—they are Earth's Mightiest Heroes from a world on the brink of destruction!

ORIGINS

On this particular parallel Earth, General Nick Fury was tasked by the U.S. President to assemble a group of heroes entrusted with defending the world. With a budget of $150 billion at his disposal, Fury set about creating the Ultimates, a team of super-powered operatives who would later thwart what he believed was a clandestine alien plot to take over the planet! The Ultimates soon recruited a lineup that mirrored the Avengers' early roster: Captain America, Iron Man, Giant-Man, the Wasp, Black Widow, Hawkeye, and Thor. Fury also hired Dr. Bruce Banner to reconstitute the Super Soldier Serum first used to create Captain America. But little did Fury or Banner know that something far more incredible would emerge from Banner's experiments. Like their Avengers counterparts, the Ultimates would expand to include members with familiar names and powers in order to protect their world from previously unimagined threat-levels!

Like the Captain America of the Avengers, the Sentinel of Liberty on Earth-1610 also battled the Axis during World War II and was frozen in suspended animation—but he wasn't revived until the 21st century!

HULK TAKES MANHATTAN

Scientist Bruce Banner conducted his experiments in a ramshackle research lab in Pittsburgh. Denied civilian trials for his untested Super Soldier Serum, Banner used the chemical concoction on himself, and mutated into the rampaging Hulk! Banner raged from Pittsburgh to New York City, cutting a destructive swath across several states until he was stopped by the Ultimates. Banner's monstrous alter-ego wasn't exactly the super soldier Nick Fury had hoped for, but Fury covered up Hulk's misdeeds and gave him a spot on the team.

SIEGE GUNS

The Ultimates' covert operatives, Hawkeye and Black Widow, were the first to prove Nick Fury's theory that aliens in disguise plotted world domination. In fact, the two sharp-shooters discovered office buildings full of Chitauri, eight-foot-tall shapeshifting alien invaders who had infiltrated Earth and manipulated events since World War II!

"Crime is becoming super-crime."
Nick Fury

Ant-Man

Iron Man

The Wasp

Captain America

Thor

Triskelion

The Ultimates were initially based on Triskelion, an island near New York City. The facility also served as SHIELD's HQ and as a prison for Super Villains. Triskelion has been attacked, destroyed, and even transported to the Iranian desert!

Ultimately, these other-world Avengers saved their Earth from Kleiser, a powerful Chitauri once active as a member of the Nazi Party.

THE ULTIMATES

#1

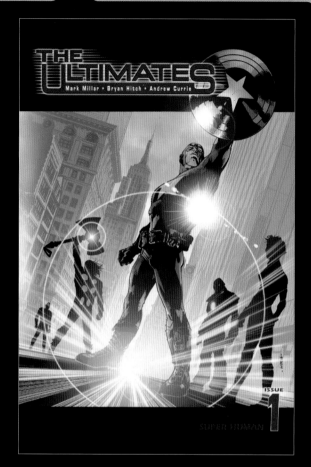

"*Don't you read the papers, pal? Captain America practically never wears a parachute. He says parachutes are for girls.*" Bucky Barnes

Main Characters: Captain America; Bucky Barnes; Tony Stark

Main Supporting Characters: Corporal Kowalski

Main Locations: Iceland; Mt. Everest

Publication Date
March 2002

Editor in Chief
Joe Quesada

Cover Artist
Bryan Hitch

Writer
Mark Millar

Penciler
Bryan Hitch

Inker
Andrew Currie

Colorist
Unknown

BACKGROUND

In 2002, Marvel Comics hoped to capitalize on the success of its *Ultimate Spider-Man* and *Ultimate X-Men* titles by reinvigorating Earth's Mightiest Heroes and introducing them to the all-new Ultimate Universe—a completely alternative reality. Writer Mark Millar and artist Bryan Hitch gave the Avengers a makeover in *Ultimates* #1, the first issue of a 13-part maxi-series that not only assembled the titular team for a postmodern audience, but also pitted them against a massive alien invasion! *Ultimates* was the first in a series of best-selling tales featuring a new world order for Earth's Mightiest Heroes. Readers were required to approach the new series as though nothing had come before in this team's history. *Ultimates* raised the bar for more mature and high-concept stories featuring these alternative Avengers.

The Story

It's 1945 and a squadron of American B-17 bombers soars high above the North Atlantic aiming for Iceland. Aboard one of the planes is a living legend, Captain America, and his best pal, correspondent James Buchanan "Bucky" Barnes. Cap is heading into enemy territory with a single mission in mind: stop the Nazis from launching a hydrogen bomb!

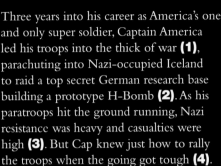

6

7

1

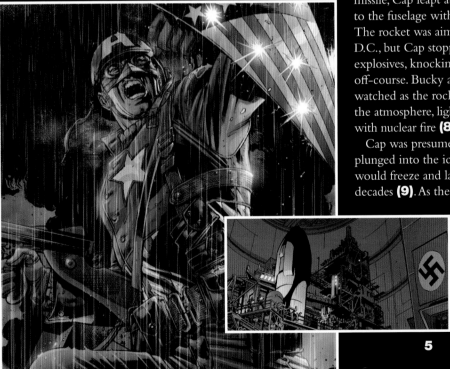

2

3

4

8

Three years into his career as America's one and only super soldier, Captain America led his troops into the thick of war **(1)**, parachuting into Nazi-occupied Iceland to raid a top secret German research base building a prototype H-Bomb **(2)**. As his paratroops hit the ground running, Nazi resistance was heavy and casualties were high **(3)**. But Cap knew just how to rally the troops when the going got tough **(4)**.

The troops were surprised when they caught a glimpse of the bomb: the Nazis had bulit an atomic warhead atop a ballistic

> *"Sorry, Bucky. You'll have to shout louder. I can't hear a blasted thing over these rocket engines."* — Captain America

intercontinental rocket **(5)**! If launched, Germany might well win the war—but not if Captain America could help it **(6)**!

As the desperate Nazis launched their missile, Cap leapt aboard and held on to the fuselage with all his might **(7)**. The rocket was aimed at Washington, D.C., but Cap stopped it with high-explosives, knocking the H-Bomb off-course. Bucky and the paratroopers watched as the rocket exploded high in the atmosphere, lighting the night sky with nuclear fire **(8)**.

Cap was presumed dead, but the unconscious hero had actually plunged into the icy waters of the North Atlantic, where he would freeze and lay dormant (but alive) for more than six decades **(9)**. As the soldiers rounded up the Nazi prisoners, grown men wept for the memory of Captain America, whose final words were discovered as a "last letter" meant for his fiancée should he perish in combat **(10)**.

9

5

10

MARVEL ZOMBIES

On the parallel Earth-2149, the Sentry arrived carrying a deadly zombie plague. The Avengers attempted to stop him, but soon found themselves infected. The plague drove them to eat flesh and before too long, the entire planet was engulfed in a superpowered zombie apocalypse. After a zombified Hulk bit the Silver Surfer's head off, a zombie Hank Pym helped to defeat and eat Galactus. With the zombies now enhanced by Galactus's energy, they left Earth to seek new worlds and life-forms to consume.

As the zombie plague erupted, the Silver Surfer arrived to herald the news that the planet would be destroyed by Galactus! The undead Avengers responded by consuming the Surfer and gaining the power cosmic.

The Wasp was "killed" when husband Giant-Man bit her head off. Her undead head was attached to a robotic body, but she was cured of her zombie hunger; She later resumed her flesh-eating ways...

"Colonel" America bit Spider-Man to spread the zombie infection. Colonel America gained the power cosmic after eating the Silver Surfer and was later killed by a zombie Red Skull. But death is never permanent when one is undead...

Iron Man lost his legs to the Silver Surfer and left the food-depleted Earth with other cosmically-powered Marvel Zombies after consuming the Surfer. He returned to find that the Black Panther had solved the food shortage through cloning!

Colonel America, Giant-Man, Hulk, Iron Man, Luke Cage, and Spider-Man returned to Earth after a 40-year rampage across the galaxy. While they were away, a group of human survivors led by the Black Panther had helped rebuild society in the Panther's homeland of Wakanda. The return of the cosmic zombies spelled disaster for the humans until survivors of Magneto's Acolytes sent the zombies to an alternative dimension.

One of the longest holdouts of the zombie plague, Thor eventually succumbed, infected by Reed Richards, who believed the best option for them all was to find a new dimension to feast upon!

Fearing that the voracious Marvel Zombies would soon use up all available human food, a zombified Hank Pym turned to giant size and attempted to eat the Black Panther!

THE HOUSE OF

It was a year after the Avengers were disassembled by one of their own, the Scarlet Witch. The team had disbanded and a shattered Wanda Maximoff was left in the care of her father, Magneto. Until... her deteriorating mental state remade reality in favor of mutantkind!

Earth's ruling family, the House of Magnus, included Magneto and his "human" daughter Wanda, Wanda's twin sons, her brother Pietro, and their step-sister Lorna Dane.

BROKEN

Taken to the ruins of the island nation of Genosha, the Scarlet Witch underwent psychic therapy under Professor Charles Xavier. Xavier, however, was unable to heal Wanda's broken mind and in order to prevent her from wreaking further chaos, she was kept under heavy sedation. Xavier traveled to New York City in order to call upon his X-Men and Earth's Mightiest Heroes to debate Wanda's fate. Should she die for her crimes, and to prevent further destruction? Both teams returned to Genosha with Xavier to see the Scarlet Witch for themselves. Unfortunately, she was gone… and so were Magneto and Wanda's brother Pietro (Quicksilver). And then reality changed! The heroes awoke in a world they would soon believe was Magneto's making, rendered fully real by his daughter's chaos magicks. At first, however, none of them realized just how much reality had changed—for their hearts' desires were fulfilled, and mutants ruled an Earth where *homo sapiens* were the minority.

In the new reality, crimelord Wilson Fisk (the Kingpin) employed several assassins including Bullseye, Typhoid Mary, Elektra, and Gladiator to battle the Avengers.

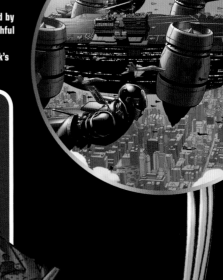

SHIELD's Red Guard—led by Wolverine—kept a watchful eye over the humans sequestered in New York's Hell's Kitchen.

Wolverine

Wolverine was the first hero to wake up and find the world around him radically changed from the Earth he knew. Having been mind-wiped so many times he couldn't remember his own age or who his parents were, the Wolverine of this new reality suddenly remembered every moment of his life… including the seconds before reality altered. Fleeing from the SHIELD he now led, he went in search of Charles Xavier, hoping that Professor X could make sense of what happened.

THE RESISTANCE

A gathering of now-human Avengers revealed that many led idyllic lives in this new reality. Peter Parker was married and had a son with Gwen Stacy, murdered in her previous life. X-Men's Cyclops and Emma Frost were happily married. Fleeing human-hunting Sentinels, the heroes discovered that young mutant Layla Miller possessed the power to make others remember the world before it changed. Layla made them recall who they were before reality shifted… so they split into three teams for an assault on Magneto and the House of Magnus.

NO MORE MUTANTS

As the heroes battled the House of Magnus, Dr. Strange confronted the Scarlet Witch. She revealed that it was Quicksilver—not Magneto—who had convinced her to remake reality to create a utopia for mutantkind. But Wanda realized that the only reality that would give her family peace was one without *homo superior*. "No more mutants!" she said. Reality reverted to its original state. The X-Men discovered, to their horror, that the Scarlet Witch had suppressed the mutant gene in hundreds of thousands of their kind, depowering 90 per cent of mutants, including Magneto. The fallout of this act would be felt for some time in the "restored" reality.

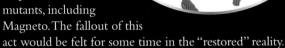

"You've desroyed everything and everyone! And used my name to do it!"

MAGNETO

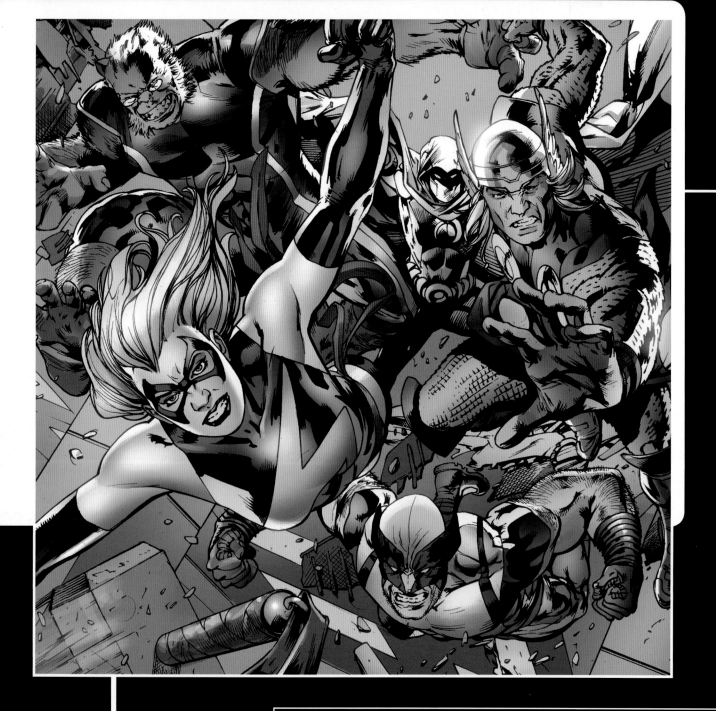

2010-

By 2010, the Avengers had never been more prominent in the Marvel Universe. With a movie in the works, more Avengers titles than ever were published. The heroes were also at the forefront of Marvel's new Heroic Age!

The end of the first decade of the 21st century was a troubled time for the world. With wars and financial meltdown making the headlines, times were tough. The changing world order was reflected in the Marvel Universe, with corrupt businessman (and ex-Green Goblin) Norman Osborn becoming the major villain. After his downfall in *Siege*, he went from government player to outright villain, but still managed to form another version of the Dark Avengers. Steve Rogers had replaced Osborn as the government's Super Hero liaison, giving the various Avengers teams one overall controlling figure for the first time. Creatively, writer Brian Michael Bendis was still one of the major players in the Marvel Universe, working on two relaunched books: *The Avengers* and *New Avengers*, illustrated by John Romita Jnr. and Stuart Immonen respectively. A third title, *The Secret Avengers* (written by Ed Brubaker and Warren Ellis, illustrated by Mike Deodato) revealed a covert Avengers group. Marvel's Avengers line also included *Avengers Academy*, where Hank Pym, Tigra, and Quicksilver acted as mentors to the next generation of heroes...

OVERLEAF

Thor, Iron Man, Ms. Marvel, and Noh-Varr (now known as the Protector) were just four of the heroes selected to be Avengers following Norman Osborn's fall from power and the start of Marvel's Heroic Age.

Steve Rogers brought together the Avengers members for their first meeting since the end of the Siege of Asgard and announced his plans for the team.

> "Our President asked me what the world needs now... I told him the world needs what it always needs. Heroes."
>
> CAPTAIN STEVE ROGERS

THE HEROIC AGE

When Kang came to the present requesting the Avengers' help, he was attacked by Thor. The Avengers stopped fighting when Stark saw that Kang was holding a doomsday device. It was an invention Stark had planned but not yet built. Stark's future self later gave it him for future use.

THE NEW TEAMS

Noh-Varr called himself the Protector when he joined Steve's team.

Following Norman Osborn's fall from grace, Steve Rogers became the new executive in charge of U.S. Super Heroes. Rogers divided the Avengers into three teams, with Maria Hill and Luke Cage in charge of two and Steve himself assuming command of the Secret Avengers, a covert group. Hill's team consisted of Iron Man, Captain America (Bucky Barnes), Spider-Woman, the Protector, Thor, Wolverine, and Spider-Man. The team soon found itself in action against Kang, as their enemy nearly destroyed the timestream trying to defeat Ultron in a futuristic war. The Avengers managed to save reality after meeting future versions of Tony Stark, Hulk, and the future children of several Avengers, convincing Ultron to lose the conflict with Kang. No sooner had the heroes returned than they faced a cosmically-powered version of the Hood. The villain had tracked down an Infinity Gem and, before the Avengers could stop him, used it to collect them all, becoming a god-like being. The heroes saved the day, with Iron Man apparently wishing the gems out of existence.

Stark later became part of the Illuminati, separating the gems once again, having lied to his fellow Avengers.

The Protector's Kree technology enabled the Avengers to see several possible future timelines.

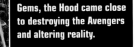

Powered by all the Infinity Gems, the Hood came close to destroying the Avengers and altering reality.

LUKE CAGE'S AVENGERS

Luke Cage selected Jessica Jones, Ms. Marvel, Mockingbird, Spider-Man, Wolverine, Iron Fist, and the Thing as part of his team. Tony Stark sold Avengers Mansion to Luke for a dollar so he could use it as a base for the team. Victoria Hand was tasked to act as the team's liaison with Steve Rogers, although her past association with Norman Osborn made the team suspicious of her. When Luke's Avengers were faced with a possessed Damian Hellstrom and Dr. Strange they helped stop the demon Agamotto from destroying their reality. Concerned for the welfare of their child, Luke and Jessica hired Squirrel Girl to act as babysitter. The team faced their toughest test when an escaped Osborn formed a new version of HAMMER.

Dr. Strange and Wong came into conflict with the Hand while trying to find the Eye of Agamotto.

RED HULK

When the cosmically-powered Hood beat the Red Hulk into a pulp, the red-skinned behemoth turned to the Avengers for help. After the Hood's defeat, the Red Hulk officially joined the team, adding some much needed raw power to Earth's Mightiest Mortals.

MARIA HILL

"YEAH, UM, I'M GOING TO HANG UP ON YOU NOW. NOT OUT OF DISRESPECT, BUT BECAUSE I HAVE NO TIME FOR THIS TODAY."

CHARACTER

The Avengers' current team leader doesn't wear a mask or have superpowers. As ex-Director of SHIELD, even Maria was shocked when Captain America—who she once tried to arrest—recruited her as leader!

Utilizing the heroes to the best of their abilities, Maria draws up scrupulous battle plans before every operation (even on the fly) and debriefs afterwards, refusing to let the Avengers rest on their laurels.

Not content to sit back while Earth's Mightiest Heroes enjoy all the fun, Maria always joins the fray, using a SHIELD-issue jetpack to keep up with her high-flying teammates.

Agent of SHIELD

In her very first appearance, Maria butted heads with Cap; a harbinger of things to come!

Maria Hill has always had an icy demeanor and a drive to succeed. She was appointed Director of SHIELD, succeeding Nick Fury, but her early command of the agency was overshadowed by Fury himself—or rather a life-sized decoy of him—who was the public face of SHIELD while Maria directed the day-to-day operations behind the scenes. Like many government bureaucrats, Maria distrusted Super Heroes and enacted policies to restrict their activities, including the Avengers reforming. Director Hill tried and failed to coerce Captain America into leading Earth's Mightiest Heroes in the early days of the Superhuman Registration Act, attempting (and failing) to arrest him when he refused to abide by the new legislation. Nevertheless, despite her contentious relationship with the Avengers, and Cap in particular, Maria continued to lead SHIELD until Tony Stark assumed control of the agency by Presidential edict, making Maria his deputy. But when Norman Osborn restructured the agency into HAMMER, a newly civilian Maria was forced to fight alongside the Avengers to bring Osborn to justice. Consequently, Maria's willingness to fight for what was right, despite what her superiors commanded her, impressed Captain America sufficiently to instill his trust in her to appoint her leader of the Avengers. She now commands the team with as much (or more) efficiency as she did the SHIELD operatives under her watch.

While on the run from Norman Osborn, Maria had a brief affair with former boss, Tony Stark.

Thanks to her military and SHIELD training, Maria leads the Avengers like a tightly-knit commando unit.

While working with Tony Stark, Maria came under the influence of the mind-warping Controller. Through sheer force of will, she escaped and completed the mission, but has suffered from increased paranoia ever since.

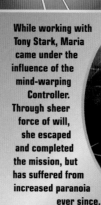

Cool, calm, and collected, Maria is adept at multitasking, a key quality in commanding a team of independent-minded heroes.

Though possessing normal strength, Maria is a martial arts expert—capable of battling the most formidable fighters.

KEY DATA

REAL NAME Maria Hill

OCCUPATION Leader of the Avengers

AFFILIATIONS The Avengers, SHIELD

POWERS/WEAPONS Like all SHIELD agents, Maria has mastered a variety of hand-to-hand combat techniques. She is an expert markswoman, and a natural born leader.

Preferred sidearm is a SHIELD-issue plasma pistol or .30-caliber machine pistol.

Maria wears Beta-cloth, Kevlar body armor, a modified version of her previous SHIELD uniform.

SPY TECH
Maria still utilizes a variety of SHIELD-issue spy gear, including teleporters, psi-blockers, hover discs, and occasionally personal jetpacks in order to keep up with her superpowered teammates.

"C'MON, ROGERS. CUT THE CRAP. WE'RE NEVER GOING TO BE TIGHT LIKE YOU AND NICK FURY, BUT I'M STILL THE ACTING HEAD OF SHIELD. RESPECT THE BADGE IF NOTHING ELSE."

When Norman Osborn transformed SHIELD into HAMMER, Maria lost her job as Director. Unemployed and unsanctioned, she nevertheless helped the Avengers battle back against Osborn during the Siege of Asgard.

SECRET AVENGERS

There are the Avengers based at the top of Stark Tower, and there are also the Avengers that nobody talks about: a secret, covert black ops team of Earth's Mightiest Heroes.

The Serpent Crown briefly possessed Nova. Cap merged with the Nova-Force to stop his powerful teammate.

THE SERPENT CROWN

ORIGINS

Formed in the wake of the Superhuman Registration Act, the so-called "Secret Avengers" were first recruited by Captain America to fight back against Iron Man's initiative to publicly unmask costumed heroes and draft them into government-mandated service. Cap's initial team of Secret Avengers was disbanded following his apparent assassination at the close of the Super Hero Civil War. Later, the Secret Avengers were reassembled when a very much alive Captain America was made the nation's highest ranking law enforcement agent following the dissolution of Norman Osborn's corrupt HAMMER agency. Cap's first act was to repeal the Superhuman Registration Act. His new team, which included Ant-Man, War Machine, Nova, Beast, Black Widow, and Moon Knight, operated under a veil of secrecy, making preemptive strikes against global threats rather than waiting for the bad guys to attack first. Opposing the Secret Avengers was the Super Villain group known as the Shadow Council. Both teams raced to locate the Serpent Crown, a talisman of great power that could be used as a weapon of mass destruction in the wrong hands.

SHADOW COUNCIL

The aims of the Shadow Council remain unknown to the Secret Avengers. The clandestine organization has made attempts to replicate the Super Soldier Serum, has mined the red planet Mars for mysterious artifacts, and has even resurrected an infamous international crimelord Zheng Zu, father of Secret Avenger Shang Chi. But their motives remain unclear. Only time will tell—providing the Secret Avengers survive the apocalypse that the Shadow Council might be readying for… or creating!

ROSTER

WAR MACHINE (JIM RHODES)

ANT-MAN

AGENT 13

PRINCE OF ORPHANS

CAPTAIN STEVE ROGERS

VALKYRIE

BEAST (HENRY McCOY)

SHANG CHI

BLACK WIDOW

NOVA

MOON KNIGHT

RANK HATH PRIVILEGES

Understandably, Steve Rogers takes his role as America's protector quite seriously. But when a zealous former U.S. soldier took up his former Captain America costume (calling himself "The Captain") and threatened to execute 419 government informants, the Sentinel of Liberty took it personally. The Secret Avengers went after The Captain, who accused Rogers of "selling out" and compromising his moral principles. The real Cap argued that black-and-white morality had no place in a society where evil existed in the ill-defined gray areas. It was those indeterminate places that the Secret Avengers were assembled to navigate.

Though many of the informants died—some by assassination and others by their own hands—Steve Rogers ended the threat by forcing The Captain to submit to the greater good.

THE AVENGERS
Vol. 4 #12.1

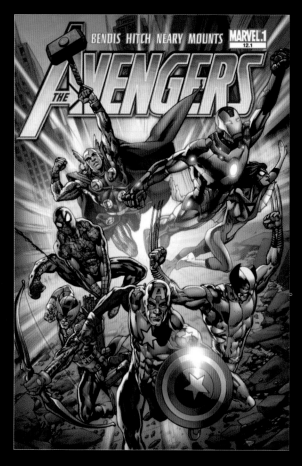

"Today the problem is Jessica Drew. I sent her out on a mission... and I think she may have run into some trouble."
Abigail Brand

Main Characters: Spider-Woman; Steve Rogers; Wolverine; Thor; Iron Man; Beast; Ms. Marvel; Moon Knight; Protector
Main Supporting Characters: Abigail Brand; the Intelligencia
Main Locations: New York City; Avengers Tower; Wakanda

Publication Date
June 2011

Editor in Chief
Axel Alonso

Cover Artists
Bryan Hitch, Paul Neary, Paul Mounts

Writer
Brian Michael Bendis

Penciler
Bryan Hitch

Inker
Paul Neary

Colorist
Paul Mounts

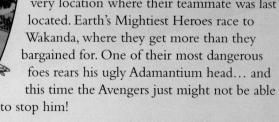

BACKGROUND

The Avengers #12.1 is one of those Avengers stories that is so jam-packed with characters that even the most die-hard fans might need a scorecard to keep up. When one of their own goes missing, Earth's Mightiest Heroes don't wait around for the villains to phone in their demands. No, the Avengers take the fight right to an all-new association of their very worst foes, the self-proclaimed "smartest guys in the room," a group of evil geniuses calling itself "the Intelligencia." Unfortunately, however, a new ally has informed the Avengers that an alien energy signature has been found at the very location where their teammate was last located. Earth's Mightiest Heroes race to Wakanda, where they get more than they bargained for. One of their most dangerous foes rears his ugly Adamantium head... and this time the Avengers just might not be able to stop him!

The Story

Avengers member Jessica Drew (Spider-Woman) was also an agent of SWORD, which gave her official sanction to hunt any alien threat to Earth, including the suspicious energy surge emanating from the jungles of Wakanda...

Deep within a cavern surrounded by spectacular waterfalls, Spider-Woman found the metallic remains of a… Spaceknight **(1)**! But the Avenger and SWORD agent soon realized she wasn't alone in her discovery. She found herself surrounded by the Intelligencia, a secret society of super-smart Super Villains that included Klaw, Red Ghost, the Thinker, MODOK, and the Wizard **(2)**! Hopelessly outmatched by the villains, various simians, and even a Super-Adaptoid, Jessica was captured!

Later, at Avengers Tower, Earth's Mightiest Heroes met SWORD's Abigail Brand and learned the true purpose of the Agency—that it deals with extraterrestrial threats to world security **(3)**. Henry McCoy (Beast) revealed to his teammates that he too was an agent of SWORD.

Meanwhile, Jessica Drew awoke naked and furious in the high-tech headquarters of the Intelligencia **(4)**. The Thinker and the Wizard attempted to interrogate Jessica, determined to learn what she knew of the Spaceknight **(5)**, while the other mad geniuses tinkered with the alien's armored remains, trying to pry out the secrets of its power **(6)**. As the Red Ghost unknowingly activated some dormant mechanism in the Spaceknight's head, the Avengers arrived on the scene, surprising the clueless Intelligencia **(7)**!

Earth's Mightiest Heroes defeated the villains

with ease, but neither team realized the greater threat awakening in the body of the Spaceknight, which arose in spasms and jerks to assume the form of Ultron **(8)**! Unafraid of the Adamantium android, the mighty Thor attempted to smite Ultron with his uru hammer Mjolnir **(9)**. Ultron himself admitted that he was unprepared for a battle with the Avengers so soon after his return to Earth as a stowaway in the body of the Spaceknight. As unstoppable hammer met immovable android, a massive energy burst leveled the Intelligencia's lair **(10)**. he Avengers emerged from the rubble relatively unscathed—compared to the broken and beaten Intelligencia. But Iron Man had a final sobering thought to offer his teammates, who were eager to pursue Ultron: this time, he feared, Ultron was destined to WIN **(11)**…

> "He will unveil himself when he is ready. And when he is ready, it will be because he has brought the human apocalypse."
>
> Iron Man

187

FEAR ITSELF

Odin's long-lost brother the Serpent, the Norse God of Fear, returned, corrupting eight powerful heroes and villains to act as the Worthy—his powerful vassals—in an all-out assault on Earth.

The Red Skull's daughter, Sin, was the first to be transformed into one of the Worthy as she became Skadi, the Serpent's herald.

Sin's Nazi forces attack Washington D.C.

◀ THE HAMMER OF SKADI

THE WORTHY

When Sin lifted the hammer of Skadi, she found herself transformed into the unstoppable herald of the Serpent. At the same time, several more hammers fell to Earth, transforming Hulk, the Thing, Titania, Absorbing Man, Juggernaut, Attuma, and the Grey Gargoyle into powerful allies of Sin/Skadi. Odin planned to wipe out life on Earth to buy time for the gods to build their forces against the Serpent. Thor objected and traveled to Earth to face the threat head on. Thor was defeated by the Serpent and taken back to Asgard to recover. Sin led her Nazi followers on a worldwide rampage of terror, killing Captain America (James "Bucky" Barnes). Thor, despite his wounds, returned to Earth to make a last stand against the Serpent.

ANGRIR, BREAKER OF SOULS

Some of Earth's most powerful heroes and villains were transformed by the Serpent into vassals known as the Worthy.

GREITHOTH, BREAKER OF WILLS

THE SERPENT

DEATH OF A GOD

Steve Rogers reclaimed his role as Captain America and made a desperate last stand against the forces of the Serpent. Meanwhile, Tony Stark traveled to Asgard to convince Odin to allow him to make weaponry that would give his allies a fighting chance. With the heroes close to defeat, Stark returned, empowering Spider-Man, Ms. Marvel, Black Widow, Hawkeye, Red She-Hulk, Iron Fist, Dr. Strange, Wolverine, and himself with weapons forged in Asgard. The empowered heroes attacked the Serpent's forces and were victorious, however Thor was killed in a last desperate battle with the Serpent.

As Captain America tried to hold the line, the Serpent shattered Cap's shield. The dwarven smiths of Svartalfheim later managed to repair it, making it stronger than ever—albeit with a battlescar on its face.

"Blood of my blood, tonight is a fine night to die!" Thor

MOKK, BREAKER OF FAITH

NERKKOD, BREAKER OF OCEANS

SKIRN, BREAKER OF MEN

KUURTH, BREAKER OF STONE

NUL, BREAKER OF WORLDS

FINESSE  **HAZMAT**  **METTLE**

REPTIL  **STRIKER** **VEIL**

STUDENTS

THE AVENGERS

ACADEMY

Avengers Academy was designed to undo the damage done by Norman Osborn's Initiative.

IN SCHOOL

The next generation of Avengers sees six superpowered youths experimented upon and tortured by Norman Osborn while he oversaw the 50-State Initiative intended to train American Super Heroes following the Superhuman Registration Act. Worried that the troubled teens might turn to villainy, Hank Pym established the Avengers Academy with Avengers alumni acting as mentors and teachers. The Academy's first class included the following young heroes-in-training: Jeanne Foucault (Finesse), a polymath who can learn a vast amount of knowledge at an accelerated rate; Jennifer Takeda (Hazmat), a human toxic waste factory, able to project deadly substances; Ken Mack (Mettle) whose iridium body makes him super-strong; Humberto Lopez (Reptil), a shapeshifter who can assume the form of any prehistoric beast; Brandon Sharpe (Striker), who projects powerful bolts of electricity; and Madeline Berry (Veil), who can turn herself into any gaseous form. The Avengers Academy faculty initially included Giant-Man, Tigra, Quicksilver, Justice, Speedball, and Jocasta.

"We're not here 'cause they think we have what it takes to be the next Captain America. We're here 'cause they're worried we'll be the next Red Skull."

STRIKER

FACULTY

JUSTICE **SPEEDBALL** **JOCASTA**

 **GIANT-MAN**  **TIGRA**  **QUICKSILVER**

Finesse believed the Avengers foe Taskmaster to be her father. With Quicksilver's aid, Finesse tracked him down and faced him in a battle that ended with Taskmaster offering her inside information on the Avengers that could be extremely valuable!

KORVAC RETURNS

While attempting to bring Hank Pym's deceased wife Janet Van Dyne Pym back from the dead, a well-meaning Veil instead retrieved the celestial being known as Carina Walters from the realm known as Underspace, where she had been hiding from her estranged husband Michael Korvac. Long before, Carina's father, the Collector, sent her to Earth to seduce Korvac. She betrayed her father and wed Korvac, though their union was brief. Upon Carina's return to corporeal form, Korvac sensed her presence and attacked Avengers Academy to reclaim her and remake reality as he wished. The Avengers' quick defeat forced Carina to fetch the Academy students' adult forms from the timestream, swapping their experienced minds with their trainee counterparts' psyches. To thwart Korvac, Veil took over his body, allowing Hazmat to

apparently destroy him. Veil later quit the Academy after experiencing the horrors of war wrought by the Red Skull's daughter Sin.

SINISTER SIX

Though the trainees could defeat Korvac they were nearly killed by an all-new lineup of the Sinister Six. While trying to steal a self-sustaining energy source from a French research facility, the Six overpowered the students, who barely escaped. As a result, Hank Pym radically stepped up their training regimen to avoid future catastrophes.

AFTERWORD

It was the Hulk's fault. Living in the UK and growing up in the 1970s, my first real experience of Super Hero comics was a TV advert for the Mighty World of Marvel, a new weekly that had a free 'green-skinned monster' transfer with the first issue (British comics at the time always came with free gifts on the first three issues). The Hulk hooked me on Marvel. Before long I was collecting their next two titles: Spider-Man Weekly and the Avengers while desperately trying to find shops that sold the colorful US editions (the UK versions were black and white, with the occasional green tint in the early days). The idea of Hulk, Thor, Iron Man, Ant-Man, and the Wasp hanging out together and fighting foes such as Loki and the spooky Space Phantom opened a whole new world to my younger self. Years later, as a comicbook dealer and then as an editor at Marvel UK, I got to read pretty much every Avengers comic ever made. From the original Lee-Kirby masterpieces through to the Roy Thomas era, the much under-rated Roger Stern/John Buscema run, and Kurt Busiek and George Perez's fantastic relaunch in the late 1990s, I devoured them all, little suspecting that years later it would come in useful…

This was a big book to work on and it took DK's very own Illuminati—Scott Beatty, Alastair Dougall and me—to make sure the Avengers were assembled. It was great, or even Marvellous, to revisit classic Avengers stories and see how the team have evolved over the decades. Oddly enough, when I was at school, none of my teachers told me that I could one day get paid for rereading the Kovac Saga, the Avengers/Defenders War or trying to work out just how many versions of Kang have existed (answer: a lot).

There have been great stories in the past, no doubt, but the present has to be the best time to be an Avengers fan. The last ten years have produced some amazing stories—most from the pen of the prolific Brian Michael Bendis—and placed the team front and center of a revitalized Marvel Universe. In fact, just when fans like myself thought it couldn't get any better, the powers that be let Joss Whedon write and direct an Avengers movie. Be still my geeky heart. This isn't just the Marvel Age of comics; it's the Avengers Age of comics.

ALAN COWSILL

INDEX